Contents

Preface

THAT there is a deepening interest in philosophy is evident from the wide circulation of popular textbooks, such as the volume by Dr Joad which has already appeared in this series, and also from the growing attendance at the classes in philosophy organised by the Evening Institutes and by the Extra-Mural Departments of our universities.

The reason for this interest is the desire to understand more about life and its problems. It is hoped by many that philosophy may be of assistance in fulfilling this need.

That Dr Joad's *Teach Yourself Philosophy* has done much to satisfy this need is evidenced by its popularity. But the more the book is appreciated the more it whets the appetite for something more. Dr Joad had the wisdom to base the study of philosophy on Plato and the Idealist view of the world which that great thinker represented. But the very success of this first step at once arouses the desire to know "the chief rival attitudes towards life as the history of human thinking has developed them, and to learn some of the reasons they can give for themselves"

This *History of Philosophy* attempts to do just that. Its aim is to enlighten the non-specialist, not to add further knowledge to that of the trained philosopher. It therefore seeks to link the thought of the great thinkers at every step with the circumstances, historical and social, in which they thought and wrote. To understand any philosophy it is necessary to understand what *questions* were stirring the minds of the men to whom the philosopher is directing his answers.

As thus told the story of philosophy has something to

reveal from the successive ages and from the men who sought to enlighten their contemporaries. And what is revealed, we shall find, is not without relevance to our age and to our problems, for the great questions of philosophy and the needs of our common humanity do not so greatly change from age to age.

It is therefore the hope of the author of this book that the brief acquaintance with the great philosophers of the world which it offers the reader will not prove unprofitable but will stimulate many to turn to these thinkers themselves for the unfailing inspiration which they may still afford.

JOHN LEWIS

1

Introduction : What is Philosophy ?

WHY PHILOSOPHY ?

WHEN we speak of a man's philosophy we mean simply the *sum of his beliefs*, or, as Bernard Shaw once put it : " the assumptions upon which he habitually acts ", those views about the world by which he actually guides his actions. As we think we live ; and how we live may be a pretty good indication of how we think.

True, the expressed philosophy of a given group or individual may not always correspond to that evident in its practice ; but ideas have a way of working themselves out in conduct in the long run.

In contrast to such positive ways of thinking, there are also ideas that function as a sort of smoke-screen to conceal or distort the real nature of behaviour, while others are attempts to justify attitudes which badly need some kind of defence. These philosophies are of the nature of *rationalisations*, and we have to be on guard to detect them and to distinguish them from those more genuine beliefs which are the real springs of human conduct.

The views with which we shall be mainly concerned are the opinions men live by ; and in this sense we can understand Chesterton's remark that " the most practical and important theory about a man is his view of the universe "— his philosophy.

Philosophy is not only important for the individual, it is

significant for the whole of society, providing a frame of reference and a world outlook which gives meaning to life, sets standards of conduct, and forms the basis of political convictions. A philosophy which thus serves society may be a stabilising force in periods of consolidation, or when it is thought proper to preserve the existing order, but, on the contrary, may be a reforming and energising force in times of change. Today we see both types of philosophy and they are in conflict. But we also see a remarkable and rather disquieting *absence* of basic conviction, characteristic of a time of confusion and perplexity. This is a serious matter, for as Whitehead says :

> Mankind can flourish in the lower stages of life with merely barbaric flashes of thought. But when civilisation culminates, the absence of a co-ordinating philosophy of life, spread throughout the community, spells decadence, boredom and the slackening of effort.[1]

It is characteristic of the British tradition to be highly suspicious of the theory underlying practice. Especially in politics the presuppositions and theoretical considerations are present, unspoken and unanalysed in the background. But is it desirable that they should be left unspoken and unanalysed ? The issues most in debate in the modern world are of such crucial importance to the whole human race that we can no longer proceed by rule of thumb. They have become what they were for the Greeks or for the medieval thinkers or for the men of our own Civil War : the question, first of all, of what it means for man to live *well*, both as an individual moral agent and as a social and political animal. And then there necessarily arises the second question : What is man ? We ought to be able to find the answer to this question, for we are surely better acquainted with ourselves than with the brutes or the stars. The story of

[1] J. N. Whitehead, *Adventures of Ideas*, p. 125.

philosophy is indeed man's attempt to answer this very question.

WHAT THEN IS PHILOSOPHY?

Philosophy has been described by William James as:

The principles of explanation that underlie all things without exception, the elements common to gods and men and animals and stars, the first *whence* and the last *whither* of the whole cosmic procession, the conditions of all knowing, and the most general rules of human action.[1]

This is a resounding and comprehensive statement. It can be put more simply as *the reach of thought beyond the fore-ground of life situations, in the effort to understand all time and existence, and that effort itself.*

In its endeavour to answer these fundamental questions philosophy pursues three separate but connected inquiries.

1. What is the nature of reality?
2. What is the nature of right and wrong?
3. What are the grounds of valid belief?
   How do we know?

1. *The Nature of Reality*

Of course if things are simply what they seem, no problem can arise. But they are not. Philosophers, from Plato onwards, have realised that appearances are deceptive and reality lies deeper than the obvious.

Consider the physical world itself: is that as final and substantial as it seems? The world appears to be an assemblage of many separate things; but are they in fact connected, linked into a system, as science would wish to be the case? Or are they, as some philosophers suppose, manifestations of some hidden " substance ", either material

---

[1] William James, *Selected Papers on Philosophy*, p. 86.

or spiritual, some underlying or original stuff whose various modifications explain the appearances of things?

We mean by Reality, then, *things as they really are*, after all error and illusion have been corrected. There are at least four theories as to the ultimate nature of this reality.

(a) The *materialist* regards matter as ultimate and mind as *merely* appearance, or less than real.

(b) The *idealist* regards the ultimate ' substance ' as mental, and physical things as an appearance or manifestation of mental reality.

(c) Mind and physical nature may be manifestations of some *third* substance which is neither the one nor the other. (Spinoza.)

(d) The *dualist* believes that there are two kinds of ultimate reality, the material and the mental—eternally distinct and irreducible.

(e) *Evolutionary naturalism* holds that mental and spiritual activities are *functions* of highly organised matter, but do not imply a separate substance.

2. *The Nature of Right and Wrong*

This is the theme of *ethics* and is known as *moral philosophy*. It is intimately bound up both with our theories as to the nature of reality and the grounds of valid belief. But the subject is so large and important that it requires a separate volume to itself. [1]

3. *The Grounds of Valid Belief*

If we consider any one of our major beliefs, either about the nature of reality, or about right and wrong, we may ask ourselves *on what grounds we hold that belief*. Many such grounds have been advanced.

(a) *Conformity*

Conformity to tradition, to authority, to social pressure.

[1] A. C. Ewing, *Teach Yourself Ethics*.

(*b*) *Intuition*

A *feeling of certainty* based on personal insight, as when a man feels sure that the physical world actually exists as material reality; or when he feels immediately conscious of his free will.

(*c*) *Results*

The philosophy, known as *pragmatism*, bases belief on the fact that a theory 'works', that it is verified by subsequent investigation or experience, or that it seems desirable for the good of mankind. We shall need to inquire whether science is satisfied with such a criterion of truth.

(*d*) *Reason*

There are two quite different kinds of *reasoning*.

(i) Reason may be a process of deduction from self-evident truths or truths which are accepted on other grounds and not questioned. Unfortunately there is endless debate as to what, if there are any, may be held to be self-evident truths or truths which reason cannot but acknowledge. Is it self-evident, as the American Constitution says it is, " that all men are created equal " ? Those who believe that such principles can be known and that a system of beliefs can then be deduced are called *rationalists*.

(ii) But reason may also proceed by generalisation from observation of facts. Those who hold that there are no self-evident truths and that valid beliefs are based on experience alone are called *empiricists*.

PERSONALITY AND PHILOSOPHY

It may be somewhat disconcerting to realise that systems of philosophy may be approved and supported for other than philosophical reasons.

Temperamentally no two of us are exactly alike; or we

may come from totally different social environments. The philosophy which flourished in the climate of opinion of the Middle Ages is not likely to resemble that of our contemporary age of science.

Moreover, much philosophical thinking is rooted in beliefs which cannot be rationally demonstrated but which are accepted on faith. It may be argued that each individual's world view is based on postulates which he cannot demonstrate but can only prefer to alternative ones.

There would thus seem to be something *relative* in all our thinking. That is to say, it is determined not solely by pure reason or objective facts, but is relative to our social background, our temperament, our preferences and our postulates.

Does this completely undermine our belief in truth?

No; but it gives us a salutary warning to be extremely critical of the various assumptions on which it is possible to build different world views. It is something, indeed some would say that it is the main function of philosophy, *to discover and state* the most fundamental assumptions of various world views, not only in our own time but in successive historical periods, and to subject them to critical examinations.

Even if no philosophy is free from bias it does not follow that all philosophies are completely unreliable. In the first place we may allow for this bias and so get nearer the truth. In the second place some kinds of bias may actually favour the search for truth. A doctor's bias for health does not get in the way of his medical investigations, it helps him. But, on the other hand, bias may completely vitiate belief.

No system of thought must be finally appraised in terms of the bias of its exponents. Primary attention must be directed towards the argument's own merits if a reliable conclusion is to be reached. It must be tested in terms of its effectiveness in clarifying and simplifying the phenomena or experiences it seeks to explain. We shall then be better able to judge whether temperament, social environment and other forms of bias have hindered or helped the search for truth.

PHILOSOPHY AND THE HUMAN PROBLEM

Philosophy is simply the culmination of creative intelligence as it goes beyond rule-of-thumb existence to significant living ; it is the most persistent and obstinate endeavour to understand human life. World views (as philosophies may be called) are not merely theoretical systems without practical importance ; they are part of ourselves, factors in our daily lives. Philosophy does indeed delve deep to find basic principles and this has given the impression that philosophical discussions are removed from the daily affairs of men. But it is no good disregarding principles. Do what we may, principles are expressed whenever there is discussion on practical affairs. The abstract nature of an inquiry should not condemn it to unimportance. The way of philosophy is difficult, but it is the way to a fuller and more understanding life.

And therefore to know the chief rival attitudes towards life, as the history of human thinking has developed them, and to have heard some of the reasons they can give for themselves, is the responsibility of every thinking man.

2

The Pre-Socratic Philosophers

PHILOSOPHY proper, as far as the West is concerned, begins with the Greeks. Greek thought continued to be influential during the days of the Roman Empire and right through the Middle Ages, when the philosophy of Aristotle was accepted as the basis of the Scholastic philosophy of the Church. It was not until the rise of science in the seventeenth century that philosophy took an entirely new form, largely under the influence of Descartes, the father of modern philosophy.

But during this pre-scientific period, while philosophy was limited by reason of its inadequate understanding of physics and biology, it derived a very powerful stimulus from the historical context of human thinking.

Philosophy does not go on in a vacuum, as though there were certain perennial questions set by an Examination Board in successive ages for philosophers to answer. The questions asked in any age by philosophers are those that arise in a particular situation ; and *the answer*—that is to say the positive propositions which the philosopher advances—are his answers to these questions, which have arisen in his own day and age. Now, the question " to what question did this philosopher intend this proposition to be the answer ? " is an historical question, and therefore cannot be settled except by historical methods. It follows that a history of philosophy must be historical as well as philosophical. For example, to understand the philosophy of Plato and Aristotle we must know something about the history of Ancient Greece and the social and moral problems created in the course of its rise and fall.

The origins of the Greek State are still a matter of acute controversy. Homer wrote in 850 B.C. of the Warrior Achaeans of Mycenae, who belonged to a period long before the great civilisation of Athens. The City States, which were the seed-bed of Greek culture, were founded between the eleventh and the seventh centuries B.C., and Greece first began to establish her colonies in Italy and farther west between 750 and 600 B.C.

We cannot understand the Greek genius and we cannot understand, therefore, Greek philosophy unless we know something about these City States. The Greek genius manifested itself in these small communities inhabiting the lands washed by the Aegean Sea. Athens was its heart, and little or nothing of it is to be seen in Sparta. Its most brilliant season of flower was between 600 and 400 B.C. ; though a hundred years passed before the most influential philosophers of Greece came to birth and its far-reaching permeating of the world began.

The City State (or *polis*) was a small, independent community. The ideal was to have no more than 5,000 citizens, so that each should be able to know most of the others by sight and so that the whole voting community could assemble in one place. That the whole of Greece was divided up into these little states may seem absurd, but it meant that this lively and intelligent Greek people were for some centuries allowed to live under a system which suited and developed its genius instead of becoming absorbed in the dull mass of a large empire, which would have smothered its spiritual growth.

The *polis* was more than a State, a machine, it was a lively community, a sort of club, an active, formative thing, training the minds and characters of its citizens in political, cultural, moral and even economic affairs. Here the individual could appeal for justice to the whole company of his fellows ; here too he played his own part in running the affairs of the community. " It is no *polis* ", says one of the characters in Sophocles' *Antigone*, " that is ruled by one man only " ; that would be irresponsible government, for the Greeks the affairs of the community were the affairs of all. Here too were fought out those desperate family quarrels like the one that led to the condemnation and death of Socrates. The City State was also an independent religious unit, for each *polis* had its own gods who were almost entirely civic symbols.

To sum up, when Aristotle said that Man was a political animal, he did not mean at all what we should mean by that phrase. He meant that such a community is the only frame-work within which man can fully realise his spiritual, moral and intellectual capacities.

The heart and centre of Greek culture was Athens, which had risen to power and influence as the leader of the Greek alliance against Persia, culminating in the battle of Marathon (490 B.C.). Many of its finest buildings, indeed, were paid for out of the war chest of the allies. It was largely the ambitions of Athens which led to the great internecine struggle, first between Athens and Sparta, but eventually involving all the City States of Greece, known as the Peloponnesian War, which brought about the downfall of Greek civilisation. The story of this dreadful struggle is magnificently portrayed in Thucydides' History.

Yet in these few centuries this small and by no means rich people created an attitude of mind which has affected all mankind, enabling them to discover new truths about themselves, their conditions and their capacities.

The results have been unreckonable in their variety and their success, notable alike in philosophic or scientific endeavour to unravel the secrets of being, and in the ardent hopes of artists' words or paint or stone to recover a lost youth of the world, a vision of a single, undivided universe, of unrealised potentialities of the human mind and heart, of an ideal order lurking behind the manifold appearances of things.[1]

THE GREEK HERITAGE

When we examine the intellectual heritage which we derive from these Greeks, we realise that we are standing beside the cradle of modern thought. For here are the beginnings of the humanistic culture that, in various forms, has since that time spread through the whole world.

1. Firstly, this is the birth of *science*, that is to say of the attempt to give a rational account of the world free from any form of mysticism and mythology.

2. Secondly, the Greeks relied upon *reason* in their attempt to understand not only science but life. Reason for them was a faculty ministering to a strange need called a sense of truth, often so apparently destructive of beliefs on which our happiness rests that we are tempted to deny it.

3. Thirdly, they proceeded to use this rational faculty in a *ruthless analysis of right and wrong* and of such questions as political justice, the law of force and democracy.

4. Fourthly, we find in the Greeks a conscious and deliberate *exaltation of human nature*. Man, they believed, was not twofold, not half beast and half deity but one, his humanity not distinct from divinity, nor body from soul. They believed that human nature could and sometimes did achieve its destiny on earth.

[1] Bowra, *The Greek Experience*.

THE MILESIAN PHILOSOPHERS

Greek philosophical thought begins with *Thales* of Miletus. Miletus was a city of Asia Minor, or as we should now say, Turkey, on the south shore of the Latmian bay and looking across it to where the Maeander joins the sea. Here dwelt Thales, the founder of European philosophy—statesman, mathematician, engineer, astronomer, the first philosopher and one of the seven sages of Greece.

The question which Thales and his successors asked was : What is the ultimate nature of reality ? It may appear to be scientific, but in that it implied that the separation of this inquiry from religion was both legitimate and necessary, it was an important step in philosophical thinking ; as it was also because it sought to discover beneath the great diversity of nature a simple, all-embracing reality. Thales wanted to know what was the original ground of all observable manifestations, that from which everything is derived and into which everything returns, the indestructible, eternal, fundamental essence of nature.

Hitherto habit and tradition had been the masters of the human mind without a rival. Men had believed without doubt or question what authority prescribed. Hence the great proliferation of myths about the creation, myths about the seasons, about the awakening of nature in the spring, myths about death, disease, famine and fertility. These Thales discarded, substituting the first attempt at a rational rather than a poetical explanation of the world.

This revolution in thinking lifted material phenomena out of the sphere of religion. True, the Milesian philosophers sometimes called the forces they invoked ' gods ', but by the term they really meant that the place once occupied by the gods of religion was now being taken by the great fundamental phenomena of nature. As Aristophanes put it,

" Vortex has driven out Zeus and reigns in his stead ". (By ' Vortex ' we might mean the whirling atomic forces.)

Furthermore, the new approach attempted to *unify* those diverse phenomena, which had hitherto been explained by a variety of fanciful agencies ; now the drifting cloud and the falling thunderbolts belong to the same natural world as the phenomena then first observed of magnetism and electricity. Nature became for them a self-sufficing orderly universe, developed on impersonal lines, undisturbed by the arbitrary volitions of supernatural beings.

As to *what* the fundamental substance actually was, this matters very little compared with the importance of the new *principle* of explanation they all concurred in. Thales thought that the underlying substance was water ; *Anaximander*, who made the first maps and suggested that land animals were originally developed from fish, thought of it in terms of a strange indeterminate ' something ', without limit in space or time, in constant change. In the universe worlds are being continuously built up and then destroyed and then re-created out of the fragments of the old. Nothing is ever finally annihilated and nothing ever comes into existence out of nothing.

Anaximines, with less speculative daring and a closer observation of fact, reduced all finite things to the element of Air, the air we breathe—our very life. To use his own words, ' that which is our soul and constitutive principle also holds the universe together '.

Four basic principles emerge from this Milesian philosophy. Here they were first enunciated and they hold even today.

1. *Consistency*. There is a single, natural basis for everything. There is no double standard of explanation— partly naturalistic and partly supernaturalistic.
2. *Simplicity*. The simple explanation is always to be

preferred to the complex—a single force is better than a variety of separate spirits.

3. *Ex nihilo nihil fit.* Nothing is made out of nothing; and, correspondingly, what is real cannot disappear.

4. *Evolution.* One thing turns into another; out of simpler elements the more complex is made; even the world is built up out of some basic substance. Change is everywhere.

Of course subsequent thinking was going to modify and enlarge these simple concepts, to qualify and develop them into something far more complex. Nevertheless, their discovery lays the foundations of both scientific and philosophical inquiry.

ANAXAGORAS

Anaxagoras was an Ionian philosopher from Asia Minor who was born about 500 B.C., settled in Athens when entering on middle age, and remained there for thirty years. He was a friend of the great patriot Pericles, who had fought in the Persian wars, beautified Athens with magnificent buildings and was a considerable statesman. When Pericles was attacked by his political opponents, charges were also brought against Anaxagoras, accusing him of irreverence in describing the sun as a red-hot stone bigger than Greece, and the moon as an earthly body, shining by reflected light. The philosophers, says Plutarch, were causing trouble. They were explaining away the divine and substituting for it blind forces and the sway of necessity.

Anaxagoras expanded the idea of *change* or development first found in Anaximander and introduced an important conception, that of *nous* into philosophy.

1. *Change.* Basic to existence we find an infinite number of first principles, or fundamental qualities which are irreducible—such as colour, smell, temperature and the

like. Change is constantly at work in nature, combining and recombining these basic elements. Change is seen just as much in society. Institutions are not permanent—oligarchy (government by the few) develops into democracy. Democracy itself is in process of development into something else. Is there anything that *controls* this eternal process of development?

2. *Nous*. Anaxagoras held that there was a force producing stuff which introduced order into the universe and dominated the interaction of the basic elements. This was *nous*. *Nous* is a kind of reason, which knows everything and controls everything. Yet mind and matter are not sufficiently distinguished for *nous* to be purely mental; it is thought of as the thinnest and purest of things and its effect is *physical*, setting up a vortex or whirlpool of the component elements. From *nous* comes order, regularity and the development of things to definite ends.

What is *nous*? It is difficult to say. It is more in man than in animals and plants; but more in animals and plants than in material objects. It appears to be an organising principle separate from matter, like Aristotle's first mover or Bergson's Life Force.

PYTHAGORAS

Pythagoras introduces yet another notion. He is a mathematician, and discovered that the square on the hypotenuse of a right-angled triangle is equal to the sum of the squares on the other two sides. His geometrical discoveries were subsequently combined with those of Euclid.

He was also a scientist. He discovered that the earth was a sphere. He also discovered that the pitch of notes is determined by the proportionate lengths of the vibrating strings, so that a string of half the length of another one gives a note exactly an octave higher.

Numbers fascinated him. He saw that quantities determined qualities—for example (as we would exemplify it), the vibration rate of light determines the colour, and atomic weights determine the properties of the elements, and so on. This was a most exciting discovery. Pythagoras declared that *Things were numbers* ; that the cosmos was a harmony of divine perfection exemplified by the relation between numbers.

Pythagoras was also a mystic. He regarded mathematics as a spiritual discipline leading to the discovery of abstract general truths. These exist on a higher and more spiritual level than mere facts, and so the spirit is elevated to this higher sphere by mathematical study. Was it not Bertrand Russell who said " Mathematics is, I believe, the chief source of the belief in eternal and exact truth, as well as in a supersensible intelligible world " ?

Pythagoras had a doctrine as to the nature of man. Man is something intermediate between God and the brutes. Is he a fallen god ? Compared with the gods he is a mere man, subject to error and death ; compared with the animals he is capable of civilisation, of rising to greater heights. This he may do by purification of the soul, a vegetarian diet and a simple life.

If this sounds fantastic, let us remember that behind the philosophy, behind the State religion of the clearly defined gods, lay a vast hinterland of very primitive religion which was developing into the cults known as the Greek Mysteries —Orphism, the Dionysian and Eleusinian Mysteries. These cults, operating with the myth of a dying and resurrected deity and with primitive fertility cults, developed a system of secret rites which delivered the human soul from death and secured for it regeneration and immortality. The followers of Pythagoras founded a religious community which showed some kinship to these mysteries and stood for a loftier view of the soul than was characteristic of the scientific wing of Greek thinkers.

The Pythagoreans wanted to save the soul, to purify it, and as we shall see this was also the chief motive of Socrates and Plato, who derived much of their teaching from Pythagoras.

THE ATOMISTS : DEMOCRITUS AND LEUCIPPUS

Democritus (460–360 B.C.) was the first philosopher to state in unambiguous terms the view that all things were ultimately reducible to minute particles of different shapes—atoms. These are beyond the reach of our senses. Said Democritus : " There are only atoms and the void." The different *appearances* of things constructed of atoms are secondary, are effects. They are merely different arrangements of the same atoms. Rather mysteriously, as they fall through space, they are aggregated into different patterns ; this is due to the different rates at which they fall, to certain hooks and notches on the atoms which enable them to join up, to chance collisions and to the vortices which they create. In other words only mechanical necessity gives rise to all the different things in the world. As Leucippus, another atomist, said : " Nothing happens by chance, everything happens by law and necessity."

Mind or soul is also formed from atoms, but soul atoms are the finest, smoothest and most active. In man's body they are interspersed among the atoms making up his physical frame.

How does change occur ?—a perennial problem for philosophers. Democritus thought that it was due to the actual movement of atoms, on account of which novelty emerges. New and unexpected patterns are continually arising. He was strongly opposed to the Eleatic philosophers, like Parmenides, who asserted that reality itself is changeless and so-called change only an illusion.

One of the most important contributions of Democritus to philosophy is the distinction that he draws between knowledge of the senses which gives us appearances, and rational understanding which gives us the reality of things. This was to become one of the most important ideas of the philosophy of knowledge—that province of philosophy which discusses the grounds of belief, the criterion of truth.

PARMENIDES AND HERACLEITUS

We have mentioned the Eleatic philosophers. They lived at Elea, a small Ionian colony in southern Italy. *Parmenides* of Elea took the conception of matter which had been elaborated by his predecessors and showed that it must lead to the conclusion that reality is continuous, finite, spherical, with nothing outside it and no empty space within it. For such a reality motion and change are impossible, and the world of the senses which tells us that things are moving and changing is therefore an illusion. *Zeno* used this theory to puzzle us with his paradoxes of motion. If a flying arrow, he said, is in any particular spot at a given moment, you never catch it actually moving, so how does it fly? From this point of view the idea of motion involves greater difficulties than its denial. Perhaps Parmenides' theory that motion is unreal is not so ridiculous as it seems.

Some of the greatest of modern philosophers have accepted the doctrine of the unreality of change. " Progress and decay are incompatible with perfection," says Bradley. " The Absolute has no history." The Good and the rational, says Hegel, are already accomplished, all we need to do is to remove the illusion that they are yet unaccomplished. On the other hand, Bergson directed his whole philosophy against the notion of permanence, of changelessness.

Heracleitus (535–475 B.C.) was the Greek counterpart of Bergson. He argued that change was the eternal law of things. Everything is in flux and nothing is static. You cannot dip into the same river twice—the water is already different from that which has flowed on.

Heracleitus lived in Ephesus, in Asia Minor, and is universally acknowledged as the greatest of the pre-Socratic philosophers, and probably destined to rank for original genius among the greatest that the world has ever seen. While water, air and the indeterminate had been advanced as the underlying reality, for Heracleitus *fire* was the Absolute, the eternally self-existent reality, underlying all appearance. Yet it is a fire that is both ever living and alternately kindled and quenched.

If this seems a contradiction, Heracleitus would assent. For him contradiction is the central fact of existence, the spring that makes the wheel of the universe go round. " Through strife all things arise and pass away." This conflict is not between completely disparate things, but always between the opposites that themselves constitute a unity. To use two modern illustrations : within every living cell the opposite processes of building up and breaking down go on continuously. The individual is due to the interaction of the seeming opposites heredity and environment ; and so on.

Existence, then, is a perpetual change. It is not mere ' being ', it is essentially ' becoming '. We have here, in principle, an evolutionary philosophy that was too advanced for fifth-century Greece. It was easier to accept a philosophy of mind acting on matter than to conceive matter as itself moving, changing and developing. That was for a later age.

The conclusions of Heracleitus proved to have significance for problems other than those concerned with the nature of reality. Out of his doctrine of the strife of opposites emerged the principle of relativity in ethics and in the theory of knowledge. What is good may become evil, what is just may turn into injustice. There is but a relative goodness and evil ; no absolute standard of right and wrong can be discovered.

This concept of ethical relativity afforded an excellent vantage point for the later ethical scepticism of the Sophists. We shall now discuss the contribution of the Sophists to the development of Greek philosophy and we shall see how, in fact, they prepared the way for Socrates—" the wisest of the Greeks ", and their great opponent.

3

Socrates and The Sophists

IN the previous chapter we noted that in addition to the first inquiry into the nature of existence the Greeks were responsible for a critical examination of life itself, of the problem of right and wrong, of the nature of politics. All this involved the application of reason beyond the sphere of the material world. This was essentially Greek. We do not find it in the speculative systems of India, or in either the mysticism (Taoism), or the precepts of gentlemanly living (Confucianism), of China.

It was the Greeks who believed Reason to be the essential feature of human beings ; therefore it was by no means only the prerogative of philosophers, but of ordinary men. Thought became the property of all. *Plato* speaks of those lovers of Truth for truth's sake who were " possessed and maddened with the passion for knowledge ", a phenomenon found but seldom anywhere in the world.

This expressed itself in :

(a) A critical analysis of their own and their neighbours' souls. It was their resolve to weigh, to test, to probe, to spare no nerve because it was sensitive, to expose all things mercilessly to the dissecting knife of reason.

(b) The practice of following the argument wherever it led. One remembers the picture, drawn by a contemporary, of the philosopher *Socrates* puzzling over a philosophical problem. He would not give it up, but continued thinking from early dawn to noon—a man indifferent to everything but the truth.

PLATO ON SOCRATES

Plato makes his master Socrates thus proclaim his mission.

While I have life and strength, I shall never cease from the practice and teaching of philosophy, exhorting any one whom I meet and saying to him after my manner : You, my friend—a citizen of the great and mighty and wise city of Athens—are you not ashamed of heaping up the greatest amount of money and honour and reputation, and caring so little about wisdom and truth and the greatest improvement of the soul, which you never heed or regard at all ? And I shall repeat the same words to every one I meet, young and old, citizen and alien, but especially to the citizens, inasmuch as they are my brethren. For I know that this is the command of God ; and I believe that no greater good has ever happened in the state than my service to the God. For I do nothing but go about persuading you all, old and young alike, not to take thought for your persons or your properties, but first and chiefly to care about the greatest improvement of the soul. I am that gadfly which God has attached to the state, and all day long and in all places am always fastening upon you, arousing and persuading and reproaching you.[1]

Nothing in Greek philosophy is more important than the application of reason to *politics* ; for there is no subject in which prejudice and tradition play such an important part, or which is so clouded by fanaticism and folly. Where else in the ancient world do we find the cool and searching inquiry into politics that we get in Plato and Aristotle ; how rarely, through all the centuries since, do we find anything to equal them.

[1] Plato, *Apology*, 30.

THE SOPHISTS

Who were the Sophists? We know that they were the bitter enemies of Socrates, and his debates with them are recorded in the *Dialogues*. But what manner of men were they?

Conceive England without universities, without secondary education, without printed books, and you have a picture of fifth-century Greece. The highest form of Greek City State was a democracy; but a democracy is lost in such conditions. To meet the need rose the class of men called Sophists. The word means *wise men*, and had originally no bad meaning. They offered to their age what we call higher education, and this education took the form of popular lectures, classes in political theory, and instruction in speech-making—indispensable in a state where every man took an active part in politics. The lectures and discussions roamed over wider fields than those of politics and were concerned with problems of conduct, philosophy and even theology.

The Sophists were passionately interested in *ideas*, and so apparently were the young men of Athens. They came to the Sophists to discuss the arguments for and against democracy, for and against moral standards, to learn the art of rhetoric and sometimes to learn how to make the worse reason appear the better! Conservatively minded people regarded them as corrupters of youth. Many of them appear to us to have been either charlatans or men who took a perverse pleasure in proclaiming a negative philosophy or turning values upside down.

Hippias of Elis was prepared to lecture on anything—from geometry to music, from painting to the genealogy of heroes; but he is also credited with founding the idea of *natural law*, that is to say an element of right common to the laws of all countries and constituting their essential basis—an idea later to be taken up or more probably rediscovered by the Stoics.

Gorgias of Sicily was a sceptic. " There is no truth." He said, " If there were, it could not be known ; if known it could not be communicated." Yet it was one of his disciples, *Alcidamas*, who first condemned slavery. " God sent all men to be free ; Nature made none a slave ", a sentiment later to be strongly opposed by Plato with his theory of innate differences among men, so that they could be regarded as men of iron, brass and gold, the men of iron to work, the men of gold to rule.

Thrasymachus taught pure relativism in morals. Justice, he argued, is merely the interest of the stronger. Who ever conquers makes his interest prevail and declares it to be right. The Athenians when they invaded the island of Melos and put all its males to death believed this. According to Thucydides they argued thus : " In the discussion of human affairs the question of justice only enters where there is equal power to enforce it—the powerful exact what they can, and the weak grant what they must "; and to the fervent appeals of the men of Melos for justice they cynically replied, " If you were as strong as we are, you would do as we do."

But relativism in ethics may be far more than the justification of the government of the strong ; it may suggest that *human interests* present the only ultimate criterion of right so that the final moral rule becomes the greatest happiness of the greatest number.

We must not be unfair to Thrasymachus. Too often we have only the account of the views of the Sophists given by their opponents, such as Plato. They may not always have put these views in the best light.

Protagoras was perhaps the greatest of the Sophists, and he too was a relativist. He contended that both moral rules and social institutions must be adapted to changing human conditions. They are not eternal. Our judgments depend upon our education, our habits, our occupation; they are not the perception, as Plato thought they could be, of absolute principles.

"About the gods," he said, "I cannot know that they exist or that they do not exist: the obscurity of these matters and the shortness of human life are impediments to such knowledge."

MAN IS THE MEASURE OF ALL THINGS

The humanism of Protagoras is most completely summed up in his dictum " Man is the measure of all things ", which well expresses one of the most fundamental characteristics of Greek thought. At the centre of this scheme of life lay a particular conception of man's nature and place in the world. In no matter were the Greeks more courageous or more rational than in their assessment of humanity, its limitations, its possibilities, and its worth. The Greeks, in distinction from the great nations of the eastern Mediterranean, Persia and Egypt, both recognised that men are worthy of respect in themselves, and were content that they should achieve this in the only life of which they had any certain knowledge.

SOCRATES

If we wish to understand the influence of Socrates on the development of Greek philosophy, it is of the first importance that we should realise the intellectual ferment which existed in Athens in the great days of the Periclean Age. We have set the stage with the picture of the Sophists debating, arguing and questioning everything under the sun; and in the background stand the contrasting philosophies of eternal change (Heracleitus) and complete immobility (Parmenides and Zeno). The Milesians [1] had put aside all supernatural or

[1] The philosophers of Miletus in Asia Minor—Thales and his successors.

mystical explanations of the world and had endeavoured to give a strictly natural account of it. It was in this that they made the decisive step towards a scientific approach to the interpretation of nature.

It was into this Athens that Socrates was born (470 B.C.) about ten years after the battle of Salamis, and he was naturally exposed to all these conflicting influences. He served with great distinction as a soldier (a hoplite) in the Peloponnesian War. It was in the camp at Potidaea that he once stood in a trance for twenty-four hours, lost in philosophic contemplation.

He was influenced profoundly by Parmenides, from whom he derived the notion of an ultimate, unchanging order of eternal principles, Ideals or Ideas ; and by Pythagoras, from whom he derived his notion of the disciplinary and philosophical importance of mathematics, and, what was even more significant, his passionate desire to save the souls of men. But unlike Pythagoras, he did not hold that the soul was a kind of fallen god, imprisoned in the body as a punishment for sin in a previous existence. *For Socrates the soul was the conscious self which it lies with us to try to make wise and good.*

Plato inaugurated an entirely new period in the history of philosophy ; that is why his predecessors are known as the Presocratics. From the time of Socrates onwards the attempt to persuade men of the truth and to " save their souls ", continued to dominate Greek philosophy to the very end.

SOCRATES THE MAN

It is not easy to discover exactly what kind of a man Socrates was because as he appears in Plato's Dialogues we cannot be certain how much of what he is made to say is Socrates and how much Plato, his successor, disciple and biographer. Aristophanes thought he was a Sophist, yet those who best understood him believed that he was the only man who could refute the Sophists and counteract their pernicious influence. We have, however, an interesting account of him in the *Memorabilia* of Xenophon, a country gentleman and a soldier with a turn for writing. Socrates impressed him as a man of surpassing goodness, who instructed and helped men *by his conversations*.

This is really the key to the teaching of Socrates. He wrote nothing and gave no systematic instruction. He conversed. And his conversation was famous for its ' irony '; this implies a certain humorous reserve which kept him from all extravagances, however interested he might be in the extravagances of others, and also a pretended assumption of ignorance in himself and wisdom in others which considerably annoyed the Sophists, whose assumptions were exactly the opposite. He played a not inconsiderable part in Greek politics, always as a man of inflexible principle. As a member of the Senate he resisted, alone, an attempt to impeach a number of generals without fair trial. On another occasion he refused to obey a legal injunction forbidding " the teaching of the art of argument ".

THE SOCRATIC DIALECTIC

As a debater he had a special method of his own which infuriated his opponents as much as his irony. This was called *the dialectic*, which was a discourse, or conversation, in which you took your opponent along with you by means of admissions or temporary consent for the purpose of seeing where what is conceded leads. Socrates usually succeeded in showing that it led either to some absurdity or to something that contradicted his opponent's own beliefs. Then he would go back to the beginning and ask his opponent to try to put his argument again in a better way (often with no better result).

VIRTUE IS KNOWLEDGE

Socrates opposed the Sophists by his relentless opposition to their relativism. They said that what was right depended on the circumstances. Socrates said that there were certain absolute and unchangeable principles to which all conduct ought to conform. These were the highest form of general truth or universal definition. The search for knowledge of such general moral truths was the search for virtue, for such knowledge *was* virtue. If you can find out what courage or justice is, what it really is, that is all you have to do. Virtue will be yours once you really know what it is. No man, Socrates said, acts on purpose against what is best, but only through ignorance. It is not the will that is impotent but the mind that is clouded. From this it followed that no one could be good without knowledge. But, he then sadly continued, who has this knowledge ? Nobody seemed to have it, not even himself. But, nevertheless, though he found it hard to discover the good, he never gave up either his belief in it or his search for it.

The arguments of Socrates often took another form, though pursuing the same aim. He used to say : If you want your son to excel in the games, you send him to a trainer ; if a man wants to know how to mend shoes, he must go to a cobbler. To whom do you go if you want to know virtue ? Cobblers and other craftsmen know their business and can teach it. They do in fact teach it. But where is there anybody who successfully teaches virtue ? Yet how can we hope for success in life unless we are shown how to obtain knowledge of rule and standard ?

Of course he would then proceed to show that this requires a different kind of knowledge from that required in a manual craft ; it involves appreciation and value, but virtue does also depend far more on clear, unbiased thinking, on freedom from self-deception, wishful thinking and rationalisation.

The therapeutic methods of Freud constantly remind us of the endless probing of Socrates.

But just as the analyst frequently arouses violent opposition, so did Socrates. He was brought to trial in 399 B.C. for corrupting the youth of Athens and for impiety, convicted and compelled to drink the hemlock. The account of his trial and death is to be found in the *Apology* of Plato, and is one of the most moving stories in all biography.

WAS THE TEACHING OF SOCRATES DANGEROUS ?

To many of his fellow countrymen Socrates seemed to be a Sophist himself and worse than a Sophist. He made politics ridiculous, attacked rhetoric as a sham and regarded poetry as mere imaginative excitement. This did not make him popular with politicians, orators and poets. His critics could say with some truth : Here is a man who makes absurd all our most honoured teachers and examples, and who does not put anything in their place. He confesses indeed that he cannot. What must be the result of such conduct ? What are we to do if we must give up everything that holds society together because we cannot exactly justify it on a rational basis ?

Plato might have replied, if he had been able to quote Hegel, " The wounds of reason can only be healed by deeper reason." Thinking is not wrong, but it may be insufficient. If so, what is wanted is not the refusal to think, but more and better thinking. He attempted to provide that better thinking, and offered his own panacea to the ills of a sick society. What we need, he argued, is not democracy, but an aristocratic state ruled by philosophers.

To Plato's development of the Socratic dialectic we must now turn.

4

Plato

PLATO'S life was lived in the decline of Greek city life. The grandeur of the defeat of Persia was long past. He felt the failure of Hellenism and his greatest work, the *Republic*, is a ruthless and objective diagnosis of the sickness of Greek society. He lived, as we do, at the end of an epoch of expansion. When Athens crumbled before his eyes he saw that the real task was not merely to rebuild Athens but to save civilisation. His task as a philosopher was to do just this, and to do it first of all by a searching analysis of the City State and of the nature of man, and then by the restoration of *oligarchy* (government by the few). But the few were to be not the rich, not a council of generals, but the wise.

> Unless philosophers bear kingly rule in cities, or those who are now called kings and princes become genuine and adequate philosophers, and political power and philosophy are brought together, there will be no respite of evil for cities, nor, I fancy, for humanity.[1]

PLATO THE MAN

Plato was born, probably in Athens, in the year 427 B.C. His first association with Socrates took place when he was twenty years old and lasted eight years, for Socrates died in 399 B.C. Plato then spent some years in foreign travel, visiting among other places the Nile Delta, Italy and Sicily.

[1] *The Republic*, Bk. V.

By 387 B.C. we find him definitely established in Athens as the recognised head of a permanent seat of learning, the famous Academy. This was situated in the north-western suburb of Athens, where there was a shrine to a local hero Academus.

This was the philosophical school in which Plato taught for nearly fifty years till his death in 348 B.C., and his followers continued to make it their headquarters. It was closed for teaching by Justinian in A.D. 529 along with other pagan schools. The apostolic succession of Platonic philosophers lasted from the days of Plato to those of Cicero, and during its whole course there is traceable a distinct continuity of thought which is of the greatest importance for the subsequent history of philosophy.

The life of Plato contained one dramatic interlude when he visited Syracuse with the intention of putting his theories of government into practice. He was then a man of sixty. He was summoned to Syracuse to supervise the education of the young Dionysius II, who had just succeeded his father. This young man was to be the first philosopher king. Unfortunately Dionysius developed into a reckless tyrant and the experiment failed miserably.

All Plato's writings have been preserved for us. They comprise the famous *Dialogues*, the *Laws*, the *Republic* (also in dialogue form), and the *Letters*.

In the *Dialogues* the position of chief speaker is assigned to Socrates, though in three of the later ones he recedes into the background. In the *Laws* he disappears altogether.

Plato never produced a systematic exposition of his ideas, though many philosophers have, mistakenly, done this for him. But whenever any eminent scholar has converted Plato into a respectable professor, by providing him with a coherent system, we quickly find that Plato in his *Dialogues* has written up most of the heresies from his own doctrines.

His influence has been enormous. The safest general

characterisation of European philosophy is to say that it consists of a series of footnotes to Plato.

Platonism entered Christian thought first through Origen and again as Neo-Platonism through Augustine. It profoundly affected the Hellenised Judaism of Alexandria, and of course it was the foundation on which Aristotle built. The most remarkable revival of Platonism took place in the Italian Renaissance, when his works were for the first time made known to the civilised world. The Cambridge Platonists in Britain arose in the middle of the seventeenth century and made their mark on the thought of the period. Blake, Wordsworth and Shelley were Platonists, and, in our own day, the poet Robert Bridges.

PLATO AND THE DECLINE OF ATHENS

Plato is essentially the philosopher of the decline and fall of Athens. We find him politically embittered by the great civil wars of 431 and onwards, but philosophically serene. He had seen democratic Athens put Socrates to death. At the age of 29 he had witnessed the fall of the city.

Philosopher though he was, he did not consider himself to be above the battlefield. The Greek thinkers never retreated into their ivory towers ; they were not too squeamish or cultured to take part in the political struggles of their day. They were citizens, and knew it and were proud of it. Political problems, they felt, were caused by man, by the interaction of human wills and desires ; and by men, by the conscious and deliberate application of human intelligence, they could and must be solved. They did not think it decent, therefore, to abandon public affairs to Providence, or to turn them over to the tender mercies of the ignorant and less scrupulous demagogue or doctrinaire.

Plato, therefore, endeavoured to think like a citizen. He faced the whole issue, and the worse the situation appeared to him, the more drastic the remedies he proposed. He was the least in the world like the pure philosopher lost to all considerations of place and time.

PLATO'S PHILOSOPHY

Plato's philosophy was not a series of reflections on certain abstract problems. He spoke in the midst of his world and to living, arguing, men. The failure of Greek political life led him to three profound philosophical conclusions.

1. Ideals do not prevail through the mere power of reason and persuasion, because the ruler is himself a divided personality. There is evil within him as well as the great emancipating power of reason. That evil is rooted in the spirit, not in the body, and what is needed is a spiritual discipline to set it free from its baser elements. The *Republic* is not merely a political tract; it is an allegory of the government of a man's own soul: Is it to be ruled by the aristocracy of reason, or by the militant force of his active powers, or is man to be pulled hither and thither by the undisciplined democracy of his instincts?

2. Not all men can achieve by the victory of reason emancipation from passion. Therefore virtue is only possible for the *élite*. Plato has no message for the mass of ordinary people.

3. The great lesson of reason, the unique discovery of the elect, and the guiding principle behind their rule is that the temporal, the many, the multifarious particulars of every day, are of inferior worth, less than real. The eternal principles which should rule the world, unchangeable, authoritative, final, are lifted far beyond appearances, and known only to philosophers.

Two conclusions follow. Firstly, the perfection and order which are lacking in the real world, on the plane of history, is projected onto the eternal. Plato invokes the cosmic to rectify the evils of society. Secondly, and more practically, since the right is eternal and unchangeable, social health is to be found by *stabilising* society, by anchoring it to the Absolute. As a famous Duke of Cambridge once said : " Any change, at any time, for any purpose, is highly to be deprecated." All social change, thought Plato, must be for the worse, must be a decline from perfection. If a state is to be free from evil *it must not change*. Therefore Plato's philosophy is a search for principles of right, of justice, of truth, of social organisation, which are absolute. Let them be found, and let the institutions and laws of the state be *pegged* to them and you will have a perfect society.

THE REPUBLIC

Through all the centuries Plato's *Republic* continues to hold its own as a perennial source of inspiration and intellectual light. It is a large book and covers an immense range of topics, though its theme is unitary and clear. It has been most variously interpreted and in contradictory ways. Readers not only differ as to its meaning but they select and lay emphasis on quite different sections. A brief exposition of the whole book is therefore impossible. What can be done is to indicate the intention of the book and the way that plan is worked out, and then to draw attention to a few of those contained themes which to many seem to have a value of their own apart from their place in the argument.

WHAT IS JUSTICE ?

The *Republic* is an inquiry into the meaning of ' Justice '. It will appear that justice is not anything that we should recognise by the word, but appertains to the city, to society. It is the right ordering of the state, with every man keeping his appointed place. Men are of different kinds. Their innate qualities vary. Some are inferior and fit only for manual work. Some are superior and should rule. A just

state requires the willing submission of the lower orders to
those ordained to rule over them.

Hence the organisation and control of the state must be
in the hands of an *élite*, with duties and responsibilities, but
enjoying no privileges and living a hard and exacting life.
These he calls the ' Guardians '. They are the philosopher
kings ; and a good part of the *Republic*, and one of the
most interesting parts, is devoted to a lengthy account of
their selection, education, higher training and testing. When
appointed they should own no property and be without
money.

Plato has some wise words on good rulers.

That city wherein those who are to rule are least anxious
for office must have the best and most stable constitution.
When office becomes a thing to be fought for, civil and
internal strife destroys the combatants and the whole state
with them.

THE NOBLE LIE

In order to get men to acquiesce in this rigid caste system
they must be told what he calls a ' noble ' lie, that is to say
a propaganda story. This is his myth of Blood and Soil,
which he calls " a handy lie to persuade the rest of the city "
to accept the rule of the *élite*. And here is the myth : " God
has put gold into those who are capable of ruling, silver
into the administrators, and copper and iron into the peasants
and other producing classes." Now any admixture of a
lower metal must be excluded from the higher classes.
" The city shall perish when it is guarded by iron and copper ",
that is to say, if it is governed by the lower classes.

What this amounts to is that men must be taught that
justice is inequality, and one of the noblest virtues after justice
is ' temperance ', and what is temperance ? Temperance is
being satisfied with your lot !

THE ANALOGY OF MAN

Just as Dante's *Divine Comedy* is not only a cosmic picture of the great figures of history suffering in hell, being redeemed in purgatory and enjoying the bliss of paradise, but an allegory of the individual soul's pilgrimage through the levels of the spiritual life, so the *Republic*, it is important to understand, is not merely a book on political theory, but a treatise on the soul of man. For in every man are the baser elements of iron and copper, the instinctive side, and, on the other hand, the element of gold, the rational side. Now just as the wise should rule the city so should reason rule the passions. Man's task is to secure justice and temperance in himself; that is to say, the harmonising of the conflicting elements in the personality under the guidance of reason.

PLATO AS A RATIONALIST

A profound philosophical conception emerges here. It can be put in two ways:

1. In training the guardian he must be taught to perceive principles, general ideas, absolute and unchangeable standards. His mind must be lifted, by education, from appearances to reality, from particular things to general laws.
2. Thus the main task of reason is to seek for those principles or general ideas which give us unity, intelligibility and *reality*. We may then use the universal to explain the more particular.

There are many important truths here, but if we restrict our interest for the moment to science, we see that Plato teaches us to pass beyond the experimental data to the general law which explains them, to the unifying and explanatory theory. Now the facts are *observed*, but the general law or theory is not observed, it is inferred, it is discovered by reason.

DO GENERAL IDEAS EXIST IN THEMSELVES?

This raises a profound problem? Plato seemed to hold that all general ideas, principles and ideals have an existence independent of the perceiving mind. We do not *make* them, we *find* them. If so, then the soul has not only a faculty for perceiving material things, but a higher faculty for inferring, or perceiving, or discovering such general ideas as Whiteness, Temperance, Justice, and so on.

THE MYTH OF THE CAVE

Throughout the Platonic dialogues we come across, from time to time, certain illustrative allegories or myths. They are of surpassing interest and great importance. We find three or four of these in the *Republic*. The most interesting is the myth of the cave. The best of Plato is not only good philosophy but good literature and the Myth of the Cave is pure poetry.

We are to imagine a deep cave with a wide entrance. We enter the cave and come first to a fire and then to a low platform on which men pass to and fro carrying utensils of various kinds. Facing this wall, with their backs to the figures moving on the platform, there are men so bound that they cannot turn their heads, and thus they can see nothing but the shadows on the wall. We are to suppose that these prisoners have always been in this plight and that they take the shadows for realities, not knowing them to be shadows. If one of them be liberated, he will be distressed by the direct glare of the fire and at first will be unable to realise that the men moving on the platform are real and that the things which he had seen formerly were only shadows. Advance in knowledge involves pain, and the

learner will be disposed to renounce the truth now revealed
to him and to return to his former bonds and to experiences
less unfamiliar. But suppose instead that he is dragged out
of the cave up the steep and rugged path into the daylight.
His eyes will be worse dazzled than ever, and, to begin with,
he will keep them on the ground. First he will begin to
make out shadows and reflections ; next he will look up and
be able to apprehend their originals ; finally he will see the
sun in all its glory.

We leave the interpretation of this parable to the reader,
which is how to treat every parable as masterly as the Myth
of the Cave.

THE THREE CITIES

The next part of the *Republic* is an account of what happens
if a city governed by an aristocracy has the misfortune to
see its rulers stray from the right path, because their character,
that is to say their philosophic knowledge, is unreliable.
Plato shows that they will decline from an aristocracy to a
plutocracy, to a city governed by the rich.

All the evils of states, and their ultimate ruin, spring from
the union of power with property, the acquisitive spirit in
high places. This splits the city into rich and poor and
breeds class war.

Out of this struggle emerges the Democratic State for
which Plato has no use at all, for it is merely the battleground
upon which two nations, the rich and the poor, fight out
their differences, and in which Jack is as good as his master.
Democratic government, therefore, cannot last but must
inevitably end in the seizure of power by gangsters.

Plato is saying that social change from a balanced, well-
ordered society ruled by an *élite* must be for the worse. He
is also saying that the driving force of decline is class war
fomented by the antagonism of economic class interests.

This whole section makes exciting reading. It is full of

a rich, if somewhat cynical, wisdom, and the parallel with our own times is often painful and instructive.

The thoughtful reader will soon find that once again the whole story is more than a political tract. It is an account of the decline of the soul of man. Thus in the aristocratic state each citizen possesses the virtues of aristocracy. The plutocratic man is the slave of his cupidity. The democratic man is pulled this way and that by the anarchy of his desires. In a corrupt society all the inhabitants participate in the defects of the whole and are permeated by its evil spirit. Again a searching lesson for every age.

Plato, coming back to the theory enunciated earlier, insists that the only well-governed city, the only stable society, is one in which Reason, in the person of philosopher-kings, rules. There is an inner principle, a goal of social and individual life working itself out in society. Discern it, imagine it, reason your way into it. It is the evolution of the Just Order, and at the same time it is the realisation of our true nature.

Plato concludes his arguments on a pessimistic note. The questioner of Socrates asks : Shall we ever see on earth a city like this ? Or is it a city whose being is in ideas only, which cannot have any real existence here ? To which Socrates replies : " Perhaps it is laid up in heaven as a pattern for him who wills to see, and seeing, to found such a city in himself. Whether it exists anywhere or ever will exist, is no matter. His life will be an expression of the laws of that city above, and of no other."

PLATO AND THE MORAL LAW

In many of the dialogues Socrates discusses the basis of the moral law, of the distinction between right and wrong.[1] In the *Republic* the Sophist Thrasymachus contends that right

[1] In the *Dialogues*, with certain exceptions, we may assume that it is Plato himself who speaks with the voice of Socrates.

is the law of the stronger.   Law is man made and arbitrary.
It is not inherently right.   That being so, man may pursue
his self-interest with impunity.   Socrates tries to show that
successful rule is not merely the imposition of the will of
the ruler, because a society can only hold together if its
members avoid injustice to one another, and this is what
government ensures.   Socrates' argument here is confusing
and not helpful and ends by a confession that he still does
not know what justice means.

In the *Euthyphro* the question is raised as to whether right
is right because the gods will it, or whether the gods will
it because it is right.   In other words, does right exist in
itself, or does it require to be derived from some supernatural
authority ?   Plato argues that the divine authority would
only have validity if the gods were good ; but it would be
arguing in a circle to say that they must be good because
they command what is right !   Therefore when we say that
the gods are good we attribute to them a quality which we
know separately ;   otherwise the statement would be meaningless.   The only alternative would be to adopt the points
of view of Thrasymachus and define goodness as what
omnipotence decrees ;   in which case there may well be, as
indeed there has been historically, a clash between conscience
and the Divine command.

In the *Symposium*, one of the most delightful and interesting
of the dialogues, the main theme of which is love, there is
a remarkable speech by the reckless and traitorous young
politician, soldier and play-boy, Alcibiades, in which he confesses that Socrates is the only man in the world who can
make him ashamed of himself ;   and so he does all he can
to avoid him.   There are times, he says, when he wishes
him dead, and yet he knows that if he did die his distress
would be unbearable.

That Socrates was a great moral teacher stands out
supremely in his trial.   When his judges command him to

be silent and to cease arguing with youth, he refuses. He is condemned to death and these are his last words to the court:

When my sons grow up, gentlemen, if you think that they are putting money or anything else before goodness, take your revenge by plaguing them as I plagued you; and if they fancy themselves for no reason, you must scold them just as I scolded you, for neglecting the important things and thinking that they are good for something when they are good for nothing. If you do this, I shall have had justice at your hands, both I myself and my children.

Now it is time that we were going, I to die and you to live; but which of us has the happier prospect is unknown to anyone but God.

5

Aristotle

IN Raphael's great painting in the Vatican known as *The
School of Athens*, the figure of Plato is seen pointing to the
heavens, while *Aristotle* points downwards to the earth.
That indeed is the real difference between them. Plato is a
transcendentalist, he seeks ever those eternal truths which
exist in their perfection above this mundane world. Aristotle
is a realist, he looks at the world around and though he too
seeks for principles, essences, general ideas, 'forms' as he
calls them, he locates these, *in the actual world*. Hence Aristotle
proceeds to a thorough examination and classification of
things. Here he writes as scientist, as biologist. When he
comes to politics, he deals with the working constitutions of
existing states. This difference between the abstract approach
of Plato and the concrete approach of Aristotle is apparent in
Plato's love for mathematics as compared with Aristotle's
biological interests. Mathematics can all be worked out in
one's head, and its truths may be known independently of
experience; Biology requires the careful observation of actual
animals. Biology, too, offers more suggestions for the understanding of the living world of men than does the rigid,
unchanging world of numbers and geometry. Again, unlike
Plato, who rather scorned the things of sense, and spoke con-
temptuously of 'the blind eye and the echoing ear', Aristotle
persuaded the Greeks that the world was worth taking notice
of. He was the first of Greek philosophers and gentlemen

to see that everything in the world was good to know and worthy to be spoken of.   This was his great discovery.

HIS LIFE

He was born in 385 B.C. at Stagirus in Chalcis, on the north-eastern coast of Greece.   He was not an Athenian, but an Ionian, and he was strongly influenced by Ionian science and the Milesian philosophers, especially by the system of Demo-critus (Atomism).   That is why he is so unsympathetic to the Western schools of philosophy, and especially to the followers of Pythagoras and Parmenides.

At the age of eighteen he was sent to Athens for higher education in philosophy and science, and entered the famous Platonic Academy, where he remained under the powerful influence of Plato until the death of his master in 347.

In 342 Aristotle removed to the Macedonian coast, where he received the position of tutor to the young Alexander, afterwards Alexander the Great, then a boy of thirteen.   The association of the great philosopher and the great king as tutor and pupil has naturally struck the imagination of later ages.   It is, however, improbable that Aristotle's influence counted for much in forming the character of Alexander.

In 335 Aristotle severed his connection with the Academy and opened a rival institution in the Lyceum, or gymnasium attached to the Temple of Apollo Lyceus.   From the fact that his instruction was given in the *peripatos* or covered portico of the gymnasium the school has derived its name of Peripatetic.

On the death of Alexander, who had conquered the whole of Greece and united the hitherto independent City States under his Empire, there was a brief but vigorous agitation against the Empire and in favour of independence.   It came to nothing, but Aristotle naturally fell a victim and was charged with impiety.   As condemnation was certain, the philosopher withdrew to Chalcis, the mother city of his native Stagirus.   Here he died in 324 B.C.

THE WORKS OF ARISTOTLE

We possess the groundwork, probably outline notes or summaries, of his lectures in the Lyceum. They cover the whole field of biological science, physics and astronomy, ethics, politics and metaphysics. He also wrote extensively on logic, and his system was for centuries the accepted method of thinking common to all science. Psychology was included under physics. It is in Aristotle that we find the first attempt in a systematic way, to give an account of the nature of art and to outline a philosophy of the beautiful.

The immense influence of the Aristotelian system, comprehensive, erudite, profound and illuminating, continued for centuries, was lost in Europe during the Dark Ages, but kept alive by the Arabs, and finally reached Europe again during the twelfth century and became, in a modified form, the official doctrine of the Church. In the twentieth century, starting in the University of Louvain, there has been a great and scholarly revival of the Thomist (Catholic) version of Aristotle, and his influence in the modern world is still considerable.

ARISTOTLE'S DOCTRINE OF GENERAL IDEAS

Aristotle opposed Plato in avoiding everything transcendental. He believed in general ideas, which he called forms or essences, but he did not agree that they could exist in themselves. Form was always the form of matter of some kind, the essence was always *in* some object, giving it its nature and properties. Thus Plato's duplication of the real world was rendered unnecessary. It was not a case of mental ideals or principles, which descend and embody themselves in real things or persons, as though Courage could exist in itself and then enter the soul of a courageous man.

Aristotle's doctrine of *essences* or forms or ideals is, of course, the basis of all classification. Seeking for the common property of *dogs*, for instance, we are able to define the species. This is the basis of logic, since we can argue from the known properties of anything: If one of the characteristics of mammals is that they have four legs, if we are told that a particular animal is a mammal we shall conclude that it has four legs. If all men are mortal, then, if Socrates is a man, then Socrates is mortal. Thus we come to the syllogism, which is the basis of deductive reasoning.

The doctrine of essences is the basis of Aristotle's theory of *potentiality*. The essence or form of a thing may be buried in it as, for instance, the potentiality of an acorn to grow into an oak. This then becomes the internal source of its development. The oak in its developed form is the complete manifestation of the form or ideal originally latent in the seed.

This important doctrine implies that *every ideal has a natural basis and everything natural has an ideal development*.

THE RIGIDITY OF THE ESSENCE

Under certain circumstances, and indeed over a wide field of observed phenomena, the doctrine of fixed essences and potentiality is most valuable and does enable us to say what a thing *is* in its essence, thus providing the basis of definition.

But under other circumstances and over a wider field the notion is untrue. Evolution contradicts it. Darwin showed that one species can turn into another (*The Origin of Species*), and even that in the course of evolution fish have changed into amphibia, amphibia into reptiles and reptiles into mammals. This breaks down the rigidity and unalterableness of Aristotle's doctrine of forms and potentiality.

It is also of importance politically and in ethics. Democracy may not be as straightforward and easily definable a category as we suppose. It may be a rather vague description of certain shifting and temporary political forms, so that what was 'democracy' for Aristotle could hardly be recognisable as such today, nor would Aristotle recognise our democratic systems as an example of what he meant by the word.

Then, again, is *human nature* something fixed, or does it too develop and change? Is development merely the unfolding of what is already there in essence, or does it go on to unpredictable goals and endless novelty as Bergson believed?

THE FIRST CAUSE

Aristotle's doctrine of the First Cause is important for theology. We often use the idea as meaning the ultimate creative agency which brought the universe into being; and sometimes we say: There *had* to be a first cause to initiate the sequence of world events. Neither Aristotle nor, subsequently, the Church meant that. The First Cause from a philosophical point of view means that behind everything that moves and changes there is Something that moves all things and is itself unmoved, the unchanging background behind all that varies, holding all things together. It is therefore not the cause which is first in time that is meant by First Cause, but the originating cause of all the temporal causes, and above all a cause which is self-determining, that is to say, it is the *kind* of cause which does not itself *need* a cause. The word ' cause ', then, is used in a totally different way from the usual one; for all the causes *in* the world, and *in* the time series, *do* themselves require a cause outside the causal series. That is why the theological first cause is definitely *not* some fixed starting point in time, it is not first in that sense at all. Indeed, philosophically speaking, the causal sequence in time could be endless. What the argument seeks to do is to establish that in the universe as actually given, movement would be unintelligible without a First Mover communicating it to all things. God, as the First Mover, is therefore the one supreme, unchanging being to whose presence the world responds with the whole process of cosmic development. He draws out the series of ' forms ' latent in the ' matter ' of the world into actual manifestation. As such He is indispensable to the world's existence, but transcends it and stands outside it.

How does God make everything move ? He moves it as something we love moves us, not by pushing it, so to speak, but by pulling it. God moves the universe by the desire he awakes in all things.

Is such a God the creator ? Not for Aristotle ; for the effect of the Prime Mover is simply to lead to the development of existing potentialities.

This is, of course, a difficult argument. Theologians accept it today, but many philosophers do not. The most penetrating of the philosophers of the Enlightenment who criticised it in the eighteenth century was Emanuel Kant.

ARISTOTLE AND SOCIETY

We have seen that all the Greek philosophers were profoundly interested in society. Plato considered the ideal form, but Aristotle considered the actual forms which it took, as evident in the different city constitutions of his time, and he looks at the State in a thoroughly practical way, asking how, and how efficiently, it serves its purposes for human life.

Therefore we have to ask what this purpose is, and he tells us that the development of our moral nature, the full realisation of our capacities, is possible only in a society which has as its chief objective the welfare of its members and the unfolding of their potentialities. There is no realisation of the good independently of the *polis*, the state, society.

Ethics is thus tied up with politics. The virtue of the good life requires a suitable form of social and political organisation. Aristotle is not interested in the ideal state— any state will do if it seeks the well-being of its citizens. It is, however, to be condemned if it fails to do this.

> For forms of government let fools contest,
> Whate'er is best administered is best.

Aristotle does, however, describe the working of different kinds of state, democratic, oligarchic, and so forth; and he lays down certain principles, such as that all men engaged in trade or economic pursuits are to be excluded from politics because they are unable to live a completely intelligent life. He is also opposed to any sharp division of citizens into classes, since this would result in dissension. He did not regard slaves as a class, because they were not really men at all, but only "animated tools".

ARISTOTLE'S ETHICS

For Aristotle there are no supernatural ideals or standards as there were for Plato. "Every ideal has a natural basis", that is to say, virtue is implicit in our own nature; "and everything natural has an ideal development", that is to say, it becomes (unless stunted or warped) what it really is. So that a good man is like a good plough, a man who embodies the proper qualities of a man and does what he is constructed to do.

A virtuous man is a normal man; and since man is in his essence ' an animal with a mind ', a normal man is a reasoning man. Moreover, he uses his reason not, as Plato believed, to apprehend, after long and special training, certain distant and abstract moral ideas or principles, but quite simply for the rational ordering of life to get the best out of it. The good man is a man who has discovered in the normal functioning of his life how to be happy.

Elsewhere, as we have seen, Aristotle makes it plain that it is only in the life of society that this can be done. Man is a being who only develops his capacities by sharing in the life of a community. He does this in the family, and in the village, but these are only elementary forms of social life. It is in the *polis*, in the fully organised City State, with its governing institutions and culture, that the good life is attainable.

The State, in this sense, is the natural goal or end of all human forms of association. Now the nature of thing is seen only when it is fully developed and the nature of man is seen only when he is a full member of a City State community. You cannot understand a chess-man just by itself. Its nature is only seen in relation to all the other chess-men with their different moves, in relation to the board, and in relation to the rules of the game.

Further, normal behaviour, the full realisation of man's nature, is not independent of circumstances. It requires a sufficiency of material goods, it requires friends, health, beauty and luck, to provide the conditions for the life of unimpeded and satisfying activity.

Aristotle lays emphasis upon *the middle course*, or mean, as the way to the best life. We need to be brave, but not fool-hardy; to be cautious, but not timid; to have enough, but neither to be very rich nor very poor. Virtue is the appropriate and expedient in the circumstances. Extremes must be avoided. Such an ideal as applied to our daily conduct is set for us by the accepted moral opinion of the day, that which is most respected. It is the opinion generally current among those who are recognised as the pillars of the state, and its more intelligent and prominent citizens.

Finally the good life requires leisure, cultivated leisure, and it is the business of the state to make this possible. The highest and noblest life for man according both to Plato and Aristotle is that life of quiet contemplation whose true employment is with the things of the mind, the life of a man in love with the spectacle of all time and all existence, and thus delivered from petty ambitions and low desires.

6

Hellenism

THE decline of the Greek City States made the task of Philip of Macedon and his son Alexander a relatively easy one. The empire of Alexander extended over not only Greece but Egypt, Persia, Mesopotamia, all Asia Minor, and parts of India. From Egypt to Afghanistan he founded city after city—often called after himself, Alexandria—and settled them with Greek mercenaries and traders. He started a new epoch of civilisation. He replaced the narrow limits and restraints of the City State by the new idea of a world civilisation, with a common culture and common speech. Alexander asserted that he was divine, and his successors also usurped the title of gods when they proclaimed themselves kings.

It was the Hellenistic world created by Alexander which transmitted to Rome the message of Greece, and made possible the subsequent spiritual unity of Christendom. The cultural centre of Hellenism was not Athens but Alexandria, and here we find a fusion of Greek philosophy, Jewish theology, Eastern mysticism and a great variety of native cults. Thus the permeation of the Empire with Greek thought was accompanied by quite other ideological movements—the synthesis being known as Hellenism.

The Macedonian Empire did not last; the great kings who divided it between them were unable to win the loyalty of their subjects or to maintain their authority. Rome entered the arena, conquered Italy and Sicily, Carthage and North

Africa, Macedonia, Greece and Egypt. By 31 B.C. the Augustan Peace reigned over the Western World, and lasted for over 200 years. It offered men something to believe in and something to worship—a divinity represented by the emperor. But its slave foundation and system of economic exploitation undermined its foundations. Men desired to find peace and security within it and were exhorted to acknowledge its divinity, but, in the words of the historian Tacitus, it was "a period rich in disasters, gloomy with wars, rent with seditions, nay savage in its very hours of peace". Its ultimate decline and fall was the culmination of a long process of degeneration, and was reflected in the religious and philosophical movements of the time.

Mankind had been offered three objects of worship: the City State, the Divine King, the Divine Emperor; and all had failed. It was into this void that the Church entered in the third century. The calamity of the people was the opportunity of the priest.

In this period the philosophies of Plato and Aristotle lost their attraction. Knowledge had *not* led to right conduct, and an ethical system deriving its authority and influence from the ideal state collapsed when the actual state was revealed as fundamentally rotten. Aristotle was the last Greek philosopher to face the world cheerfully; Hellenistic philosophy reflected an acceptance of defeat, acquiescence in frustration and humiliation, a turning away from the shifting, disappointing world to find some new source of peace.

This reaction took two opposite forms:

Firstly, a rationalism which now refused to look beyond nature and experience, which inculcated a spirit of equanimity or peace of mind, which tried to show men how to be happy though subjugated and enslaved or how to endure the worst that life can inflict on man. This we find in *Epicureanism* and *Stoicism*.

Secondly, a speculative development of Platonism strangely

combined with elements of mythology and superstition, which helped to recommend it to weaker minds ; so that the same philosophy that was at its best an exalted form of mysticism became among the masses a preposterous farrago of nonsense. This is Neoplatonism.

Both tendencies reflect a failure of nerve, an acceptance of failure, the discovery that the secret of peace is not to make our achievements equal to our desires, but to lower our desires to the level of our achievement. But this reaction to defeat had a positive side to it. It was the discovery of *self-consciousness* ; and it arose out of the failure of the *other-consciousness* of Plato and Aristotle. These new philosophic schools developed from the disintegration of Greek society, but they did much to fructify the Christian religion and have been a perennial source of inspiration ever since. Their aim was to make the individual, separated by social collapse from everything which up to then had stayed and fortified him, independent of everything outside himself, and to lead him back into his inner life to seek his real happiness in the peace of the spirit, a peace which might remain unshaken whilst the whole world was collapsing around him.

THE EPICUREANS

Epicurus, born seven years after the death of Plato, lived in the period of Greek decline and the fall of Athens. He founded his school in that city and here instructed his disciples in the art of rational living. He taught that pleasure and happiness are the natural end of life ; but contrary to popular misconceptions, he did not advocate the pursuit of pleasure. Joys of the mind are superior to the pleasures of the body ; " We cannot live pleasantly ", he said, " without living wisely, and nobly, and righteously."

Epicurus taught that there was no greater happiness than that found in friendship ; but society (as he found it) was inimical to friendship, setting man against man. The institution of property had substituted wealth for personal worth and fostered a spirit of envy, enmity and competition. Hence true peace of mind was only to be found by gathering together the like-minded and trying to live, as far as possible, in independence of the corrupt world.

The Epicureans were also atomists, or materialists, like Democritus (though this did not mean that all matter was tangible). Soul is material, but exceedingly fine, and works with the coarser matter of the physical body. Moreover, Epicurus was not a determinist, holding that each atom had the power of spontaneous movement, and that human purpose and will could triumph over necessity and chance.

The Epicureans were anti-religious. They wanted to deliver men not only from fate but from the gods as supernatural powers interfering with man. This, they held, was a great source of fear, darkening and benumbing the mind of man.

Lucretius (98–54 B.C.) was a Roman Epicurean who, in his great poem on *The Nature of Things* (*De Natura Rerum*), attempted to remove the dread of death by overcoming belief in immortality and the gods.

Epicureanism was a guide for the individual in a period of social collapse. While feeling alone could decide what was good, reason must balance possible pleasures and pains. Above all we must not attempt too much, or force oneself beyond one's strength. "Blessed is he who expects nothing, for he shall never be disappointed." Prudence is a more precious guide to happiness than speculative philosophy.

THE STOICS

Zeno (340–265 B.C.) was a native of Cyprus and the founder of the Stoic School in Athens. The name was taken from the *stoa* or painted porch in which his philosophical discussions were carried on. Like Epicureanism, Stoicism found its way to Rome where it was taught by the slave philosopher

Epictetus and by the Emperor *Marcus Aurelius*.   *Seneca*, the tutor of the young Nero, was also a Stoic.

The philosophy of Zeno was built on the principle that reality is a rational order, an organic whole, in which nature is controlled by laws of Reason.   This is a form of *pantheism*, since God as Reason pervades and controls all things.   It is our *reason* which we share with God and with Nature.

But if everything is part of a rational order, everything is justified.   This is indeed the Stoic conclusion.   An immutable destiny assigns to each his station.   It is our wisdom to accept our lot and do what must be done, patiently, quietly, uncomplainingly, fittingly.   Because an evil world is beyond our control we must submit to learn to live with disappointment, frustration, evil.   This was a time " when the Phoenicians were pouring into battle on every front, when the world rocked with the shock and tumult of war and shivered from centre to firmament, when all mankind on sea and land were in doubt ".[1]   Toynbee calls it the *Age of Agony*.

The Stoic tried to equip the individual with a spiritual armament to make him invulnerable to all the slings and arrows of fortune and imperturbable amid all the chances and changes of life.

One thing more must be said : The Stoic was the first cosmopolitan.   The Divine Reason was in every man and so all men were brothers, sons of God.   Loyalty to the city was no more, loyalty to king and emperor was losing its force ; should we not give our devotion to a greater City ?   " The poet can address Athens as ' Thou dear city of Cecrops ', canst thou not address the Universe as ' Thou dear City of God ' " (Marcus Aurelius).

Stoicism inspired nearly all the great characters of the early Roman Empire and nerved almost every attempt made to maintain the freedom and dignity of the human soul.   But both Stoicism and Epicureanism were philosophies for the

[1] Lucretius, *De Natura Rerum*, iii. 830.

élite only. They required more strength of mind than most men possessed. Spiritually self-sufficient philosophers were worthier models for gods in human form than politically potent kings, but they too were unsatisfying objects of worship.

Yet through the centuries their teaching has reappeared again and again : in the doctrine of the Law of Nature and the Rights of Man, in the ideal of the unity of the human race, in the principle of a rational order sustaining the universe ; while we find more than echoes of Epicureanism in Molière, Rousseau and Voltaire. Shakespeare makes many of his characters speak ' philosophically ', and when they do so it is usually some echo of the ancient stoics. To take things philosophically is to take things stoically, or even to be somewhat indifferent both to joy and sorrow. Boswell tells us that an old friend of Dr. Johnson once said to him : " You are a philosopher, Dr. Johnson, I have tried, too, in my time to be a philosopher ; but I don't know how, cheerfulness was always breaking in."

NEOPLATONISM

Side by side with the rationalism of the Epicureans and Stoics we find a very different tendency in the mysticism of Neoplatonism. While this derived much of its teaching from Plato, it radically transformed his position, a development which was due to the profound influence of Eastern religion and Gnosticism on the Hellenistic philosophy of Alexandria.

Gnosticism [1] was a fusion of religious and philosophical ideas from many quarters. There was something of the Orphic Mystery Religion of Greece with its promise of redemption through union with God. The way to salvation in these mystery cults was through abstinence and discipline, by participation in a secret ritual, and by receiving thereby the sacred truth that God and man are united, and man is filled with deity.

[1] Gnosticism is ' secret knowledge '.

Gnosticism borrowed much from the mystery religions, and it also embodied a number of fantastic ideas derived from contemporary beliefs about the heavenly bodies which were supposed to exert a mysterious influence over man. Behind the stars were the World Rulers who fixed men's destiny. The earth was the sphere of their tyranny. The heavenly bodies were thought of as situated on concentric crystal spheres enveloping the earth, which was believed to be the centre of the physical universe. These spheres were barriers between the soul and its true home, and spiritual emancipation involved learning the way through their complicated geography, evading the watchful demons who guarded their gates. By this pilgrimage the soul rises from the fallen and earthy state of mere men to spiritual enlightenment and a return to its true heavenly home. For in men, creeping on the earth, in bondage under the celestial powers, there was something, a spark, a seed, a breath, which belonged by origin to that far-off divine world from which all souls had come.

There were various theories as to how the world and its inhabitants had come into existence ; either it was some sort of fall from the spiritual to the material level; or perhaps an evil power was responsible for the creation of the material world. In any event, men needed deliverance, and this deliverance depended primarily on *knowledge*, a secret knowledge, perhaps too some kind of intellectual illumination and the discovery of secret and potent words and names ; it also required fasting and ritual proceedings ; and, in some forms of Gnosticism, a Divine Redeemer who descends to deliver the imprisoned element of divinity.

The basic belief of Gnosticism was that Evil is connected with the transitory material world, which is the sphere of the senses and instincts. The world is a prison house from which we must be delivered.

Plotinus (A.D. 204–270) was a native of Lycopolis in Egypt

who studied and taught at Alexandria during the early third
century A.D.   At this time Alexandria was the meeting-place
of Oriental and Greek scholars, and the mingling of their
cultures gave rise to the first attempts to unite elements from
all of them into a new synthesis.   The work of Plotinus is
to be regarded as an amalgamation of Plato's philosophy and
Oriental mysticism, and is deeply tinged by Gnosticism.   He
may be regarded as the last of the great philosophers of
antiquity.

Plotinus draws a sharp distinction between the world of
the senses and the world of the mind, between the phenomena
of change and the unchanging eternal, between the everyday
facts of experience and the truth behind them attained by
reason.   The task of the philosophic man is to seek the
intelligible world beyond the illusions of appearance.   Behind the differences and disagreements of life, behind its
difficulties and unsolved conflicts, there is eternal truth if we
know how to find it.

If we call the ultimate reality God, then we may say about
Him :

(*a*) That God is *in* everything.   The relation of God to
      things is not external, they are manifestations of His
      thought.   This is a form of *pantheism*.

(*b*) God does not, however, degrade Himself by actual con-
      tact with matter.   The connection between the eternal
      spiritual reality and the temporal material world is
      through a series of stages or *emanations*.

The Absolute gives rise to *Nous*—the creative reason, and
this gives rise to the *World Soul* which produces men and
material things.   In Platonic fashion the mind is carried upwards from things to general classes or species, to ' forms '
or Ideas, and from them to the *Principle of Creative Life*, and
to the ordering principle which is responsible for the tendency

to order and to development—the movement of things to their goal or completion.

If, on the other hand, instead of looking up to the ' forms ' and principles, we look down, we only see things in their diversity and separateness and self-sufficiency, instead of seeing the higher and higher levels of classification and order which link things into a unity and ultimately reveals their existence in and dependence upon the All.

Neoplatonism is not only a philosophy, it is a way of salvation. Entering the life of the spirit we become detached from our worldly selves ; and as we rise in contemplation of more and more general truths we begin to lose the distinction between ourselves and what we know ; and as the *unity of subject and object* is realised, all conflict and opposition disappears, the soul passes beyond space and time, beyond history. This flight of the emancipated soul carries it beyond even the great figures and teachers who have limited themselves by appearing in historic time, beyond even the greatest prophets and philosophers. Finally, the aspiring soul even passes beyond God as a person, to arrive at identity with the All.

This process can be described as an ascending series of *negations*. The Absolute can be conceived only in terms of what it is not : Truth is not *this* thing, but the general idea (not *this* dog, but the species Dog), not the material but the spiritual, not the limited but the unlimited, not *this* truth but the wider truth ; not *this* wider truth but a more embracing principle ; not *this* prophet or preacher but an Ideal beyond them ; not any particular Ideal, but something more comprehensive, not that which can be defined, but the undefinable, not even God, but something bigger. What is ultimately reached may be described as Everything ; or, equally well, as Nothing.

For Plotinus the paramount pursuit for a philosopher was not intellectual work but contemplation, and the crown of contemplation was the mystical experience of the human soul's union with God.

With Neoplatonism the effort of Greek thought and of Hellenism to find a satisfactory solution for both the religious craving and the philosophical aspiration of the time came to a close. It was a way of life based upon individual training, mental discipline and contemplation. Christianity engulfed and swept over it, but its mark was left upon the thought of the time as witnessed by the theology of Augustine and the mysticism of the Middle Ages.

Following Plotinus and his disciple *Porphyry* the thought of the school underwent some marked changes, especially as regards the stages or emanations separating man from God. After a period of decline the school was revived in the fifth century A.D. by *Proclus* in Athens and was continuing under the leadership of his followers when the Emperor Justinian closed all the pagan schools of philosophy in the year A.D. 529.

7

The Medieval Synthesis

AFTER the fall of Rome there arose to fulfil many of the functions of the Empire a new and remarkable organisation—the Christian Church. Long years of discipline and persecution, the inspired leadership of many scholars, administrators and saintly persons, had prepared it for its great tasks and onerous responsibilities.

Rome in its days of decadence had proved unequal to the occasion. A confused, distrustful, greedy, superstitious and defeated pagan majority capitulated to the organised Christian minority, that knew its own mind and shrank from no effort and no hardship in executing its will. And further, Rome was patrician, the Church, though it included patricians, was a Church of the common people. No other creed was humble enough to lay its foundations among the buried hopes, fears and desires of the masses, or to give the poor and humble parity with the rich, the wise and the proud.

The Medieval Age falls into three periods. The first, known as the Dark Ages, covers the centuries from the fall of the Western Empire to the recovery of the philosophy of Aristotle, who had been almost completely forgotten. Outwardly it was a period of stress and strain, the upheaval of a world already broken in pieces. Viewed from within, the period was marked by superstition and terror. Only in the Church did men find some groundwork of authority and an element of order. Of the great inheritance of Greek thought almost nothing had survived. One personality, however, that of *Augustine*, infused into religious thinking all that Christian philosophy could tolerate of Neoplatonism —and perhaps more than was consistent with it.

The second period was marked by the discovery and translation of Aristotle and the reorganisation of medieval thought by *Aquinas* and the schoolmen, that highly trained body of scholars, who were all either monks or clerics, teaching in monasteries, cathedral schools or universities. They taught in a common language and moved freely both as teachers and students from college to college and from country to country.

They moulded the mind of the age. The result was the medieval synthesis, with its vast superstructure of theology, which equipped the Western World with an intellectual system, a world view, that embraced not only metaphysics, logic and theology, but morals, politics and every aspect of human life.

The Schoolmen created a framework of belief and dogma in which coherence and intelligibility, though often founded on arbitrary assumptions, did service for the truth for many hundreds of years. It was coherent and within its accepted principles, logically constructed.

The third period, which began in the fourteenth century, saw the beginnings of the impact of a revived Platonism on medieval thought, the challenge of the new astronomy, as presented by Galileo, the great controversy on the relations of faith and reason, and the demands of a Renaissance world in love with life, which undermined the Neoplatonic and Christian ideas of the baseness of the world of the senses and its joys.

This whole world of thought is much less accessible to our thinking than we suppose. What can the scientists, historians and philosophers of the twentieth century make of the theology-history, the philosophy-science, the dialectic-methodology of the thirteenth? We peruse with difficulty the weighty folios of St. Thomas Aquinas, we can wonder at the zest, the patience, the ingenuity and acumen displayed by the medieval philosophers. The one thing we cannot do is to cope adequately with their arguments. We can neither assent to them nor refute them. Indeed, we feel that in the climate of opinion which sustains such arguments we can hardly breathe. The fact is that the world pattern into which they are so dexterously woven is no longer capable of eliciting from us any complete comprehension of its meaning.

ST. AUGUSTINE (A.D. 345–430)

Augustine of Hippo in North Africa began his active life as a classical lecturer in Carthage, Rome and Milan. For many years he was not only a Neoplatonist but a philosophical dualist [1] in his conception of human nature, believing that though man contained a spark of the Divine, he was created by Satan in conjunction with Sin. Just as heaven was completely separated from the world, so the soul was separated from the body. For Augustine, who was an extremely sensual man, his Neoplatonic mind seemed to be sundered absolutely from his sinful body. This theory of human nature was held by a sect known as the Manichees, and Augustine's philosophy, even after his conversion, remained profoundly influenced by their philosophy and through him penetrated the Church, and especially monasticism.

Augustine was converted at the age of 32 and became the most noted controversialist and philosophical teacher of his age. The Church at that time was more a religious organisation than an ideological force, and Augustine almost succeeded in imposing upon it a Neoplatonic philosophy. Perhaps his most important task was to equip Christian thought not only with a metaphysic but with a philosophy of history. In reply

[1] *Dualism*, comprising two opposite principles.

to the taunt that it was Christianity that had undermined Rome, he wrote his *Civitas Dei* (*The City of God*) to make clear the relation of the Church to the sinful world.

Augustine also gave to the Church a conception of predestination and irresistible grace which was really a form of religious determinism. This gave to Christian men a tremendous feeling of their strength and authority in the world. Men possessed with the idea that they are predestined instruments in the hands of God have effected more than those who have believed themselves to be entirely free agents. The role that the Church was to play during the Dark Ages, the conviction that it had the right to bind and lose not only spiritual things but earthly and worldly things, and therefore the right to subdue kings and emperors, was largely due to this belief that it was the irresistible instrument of the Divine Will.

No other single Christian thinker after St. Paul was to influence so profoundly the Christianity of western European peoples. Augustine possessed an acute and disciplined intellect ; he was familiar with the best Roman thought and with contemporary Greek philosophy. He was no mean orator and a great organiser. His thought dominated Christianity for 800 years.

THE AUGUSTINIAN SYNTHESIS

The greatness of Augustine lies in his synthesis of opposing tendencies. His rich, many-sided nature appropriated from all sorts of sources, but gave a new significance to all.

1. *Neoplatonism.* Augustine did not read the *Dialogues* of Plato until he was 32. As developed and modified by Plotinus, the philosophy of Plato made clear to him that God is a spirit, immaterial, eternal, incorruptible, unchangeable, the supreme unity that is the Soul of souls. Yet this God we may perceive in mystical vision if we proceed far enough along the road of fasting, abstinence and endeavour.

God is the supreme being upon whom the entire creation depends; the universe is made out of nothing at God's desire and He is to be thought of as everywhere spiritually present. It is in God that the entire universe has its unity.

In accepting this view he rejects his former Manichean conception of the world as a *double* system of good and evil, involving the theory that man's body and half his soul are the work of an evil being. He now accepts the whole creation as in its nature good. Evil is not an eternal power in opposition to God, but the fruit of man's own folly in turning aside from God.

THE LOGOS

The Alexandrian philosophers had spoken of the *logos* or Word or Reason of God as almost a distinct emanation or creative principle; the Stoics too had thought of the Reason which embodies itself in man and nature. Plotinus had taught that *Nous* played a necessary part in the creation of man and his world. In the Gospel of St. John this essentially Greek notion appears in such statements as " In the beginning was the Logos (Word), and the Logos was with God, and the Logos was God. All things were made by him . . . In him was life; and the life was the light of men . . . And the Logos became flesh and dwelt among us, and we beheld his glory." When Augustine turned to Christianity he saw that the Eternal was not only infinitely distant, as Plotinus believed, but at the same time:

Closer is he than breathing
Nearer than hands or feet.

There was a Mediator, who had created the world, *but was not less than God*, and it is through the Logos, the Christ, that the world and God and all things, including ourselves, become comprehensible to us. Thus Augustine united in a new synthesis the Platonic philosophy and the Christian gospel and at the same time emancipated himself from dualism.[1]

SIN AND REDEMPTION

But this was not enough. If one is to do more than contemplate God through the glass of concepts, if one is to touch God and enjoy Him, to be united to Him in spirit and in truth, one needs more than intellectual contemplation, one needs to be cleansed from sin. How is this to be brought about? Augustine rejected utterly the view that any man if he wanted to could become good. Instead he accepted the doctrine that the Christian man can only be *cut off from sin* by the irresistible Grace of God, and this will only take place if he is one of the elect. The Church consists of these *new men*. It is the visible organisation of the redeemed. The redeemed man had a sense of being *chosen* which stripped him of all pride, but gave him a new dignity, utter fearlessness and boundless energy.

Augustine never lost his profoundly pessimistic view of life, which he held to be no more than a preparation for the hereafter; but he escaped the worst of the Manichean doctrine that nature was essentially evil.

A PHILOSOPHY OF HISTORY

With Augustine's view of the Church as the *City of God* there emerged a basically new philosophy of history. He saw the Church as a definite organisation *in* the world but not *of* the world. He had no vision of a regenerate human society, no utopian hopes of a better world. There was no hope of salvation in the secular state or in the temporal society, because of the inherent character of the human condition —man's fallen nature, and the fact that those outside the Church were predestined to be damned.

To serve the City of God, the Church, is the highest duty

[1] It is doubtful if he ever completely escaped from dualism.

of the State. If the State is un-Christian the Church will condemn it, for the Church claims supremacy over the world and authority over the secular state.

The world lies in the Evil One and is concerned with lower things. It will never become a redeemed society, the Kingdom of God on earth. The Kingdom is not a future society of good men, but a *present* society of men whose concern is *not* the world at all, but spiritual values.

In effect this doctrine underlay the relations of Church and State through the succeeding centuries. It was an Augustinian triumph when Gregory the Great forced the Emperor, Henry IV, to kneel in utter subjection to him in the snow of winter, before the gates of the Castle of Canossa, and in ignoble humiliation crave absolution from the Spiritual Authority who asserted the supremacy of the Pope over all worldly monarchs.

History became the working out on the plane of temporal events of a cosmic scheme of creation, fall and redemption ; it thus received a coherent, objective and unifying thread of meaning. By the tenth and eleventh centuries the Church had emerged as the dominant force for order and the chief dispenser of wisdom. The ensuing period of thought, historically the Middle Ages, is the period of medieval philosophy to which we must now turn.

THE ARABIAN PHILOSOPHERS

While the lights of learning and culture went out one by one in Europe, a richer civilisation than anything found in Rome was flourishing in Damascus, Baghdad, Cairo, and Cordova in Spain, which the Arabs had conquered and settled. In Baghdad there were 36 public libraries and a hundred bookshops. It was one of the largest cities in the world.

Thus between the eighth and the eleventh centuries, the Dark Ages of Europe, Arabian culture flourishes, assimilating the learning both of the East and of Ancient Greece. The

Arabs put mathematics on a sound basis by the system of numerals which they invented and which we use today, they invented algebra, and plane and spherical geometry. They improved such knowledge of chemistry as men at that time had, and freed both chemistry and physics from metaphysics and magic. But above all they assimilated and preserved the great philosophical heritage of Greece, the philosophy of Aristotle. His works were translated into Arabic, and it was in this form that they eventually reached Europe.

What the Arabian philosophers were trying to do was to make the religious ideas of Islam understandable and acceptable to intellectuals ; this they did by bending the philosophy of Aristotle to the service of theology, harmonising the concepts of reason with revealed truth.

Avicenna (Ibn Sina, died 1037), distinguished in medicine, geometry, physics and law, as well as in philosophy, interpreted Aristotle in a Neoplatonic manner. God cannot create material things directly, in His mind are all the Universals and these are taken over and operated by subordinate Intelligences. Secondly, just as the idea exists in the sculptor's mind *subjectively* before it is embodied in the statue, so the ' forms ' or ' ideas ' of all things exist subjectively in the mind of God. Thirdly, the universal, or ' form ', or ' idea ' becomes objective when embodied in matter when the statue is made. Thus we have the ' idea ' of man in the mind of God, and then, when man is created, ' mankind ' is actually present *in* every man. Fourthly, we can then discern the general in the particular, and abstract it by a mental process, and thus create it for ourselves, after observing the objects in which it is found. Thus the only *real* existence of universals is *in* particular things.

Aquinas practically followed Avicenna in this and established a position which refuted on the one hand those philosophers (the Realists) who held, with Plato, that Universals like Courage, Whiteness, Dog, could and did exist in themselves and independently of *brave* men, *white* ducks and fox-terriers, and from the rival school of philosophy (the Nominalists) who held that universals are *no more* than concepts formed by the mind after inspecting different objects.

Averroës (Ibn Rushd, 1126-98) was the last of the Arabian philosophers, was born at Cordova in Spain, but being accused of unorthodoxy he retreated to North Africa and died in Morocco. He is not so much an original philosopher as the author of an elaborate commentary on the whole works of Aristotle.

His exposition of Aristotle included a theory of the universe far more mechanical and materialistic than his master's. He believed in the eternity of matter and saw no necessity for a creative moment at which the world was brought into existence by God. Aquinas accepted this as philosophically sound, but believed, purely on the basis of revelation, that in fact creation had occurred at a particular time.

Averroës believed that Reason was a universal thing, it is the common reason of humanity, a sort of World Soul. There is no such thing as an individual soul, our mind is but part of the universal intelligence, therefore God is not interested in individuals and there is no personal immortality. The Reason of God dwells temporarily in all of us—a pantheistic notion.

Another doctrine, which was speedily taken up by many theologians who read the Latin translation of his works in the thirteenth century, was his famous statement about " twofold truth ", to the effect that a proposition may be theologically true and philosophically false, and vice versa.

ST. THOMAS AQUINAS (A.D. 1225-74)

The Neoplatonism which lingered in the philosophy of Augustine, and to a considerable extent came to permeate

Christian thought, did not provide a satisfactory ideological framework for theology. It separated spirit and matter and regarded the senses as more likely to hinder than to help in the religious life. It entirely subordinated reason to faith. There was a constant tendency to regard nature as evil, or at any rate as a lower order of existence somehow hostile to spirit, and to hold that all wisdom is to be found in the apprehension of purely spiritual truths; as if no part of wisdom had any root anywhere in the real world.

This whole attitude was too Platonic, too Eastern, too dualistic in its radical separation of matter and spirit, for a faith which sought to guide and inform the rapidly developing secular order of the Middle Ages. It was a philosophy for mystics rather than for men of flesh and blood.

The man who corrected the exaggerated spirituality of Augustinian theology was Thomas Aquinas. He entered the Dominican Order in 1244; studied theology in Paris and became the most noted philosopher of his own time and the succeeding centuries of the Catholic era.

Many Christian thinkers had been greatly enlightened by the Latin translations of Averroës' Commentaries on Aristotle, who seemed to them to have more relevant things to say to their day and age than the more Platonic philosophers of the Church. But it also seemed that, in the form in which Averroës presented it, the philosophy of Aristotle was contrary to the teachings of the Church.

The problem was, therefore, to restate and modify Aristotle in order to preserve and make full use of what was of inestimable value, while rejecting what was unacceptable. This was the task of Thomas Aquinas, who wrote an immense library of philosophical and theological works, of which the most important are the *Summa Contra Gentiles* and the *Summa Theologica*.

The philosophy of Aquinas, as he is generally called, rejects the notion that evil or sin is rooted in the body or the material world, or nature. If these can be misused, so can things of the spirit; but they are completely capable of holy usage. They are none of them bad in themselves.

Continuing along this line he rejected the Platonic view that intellectual knowledge does not take place through the operation of sensible objects on the intellect. For Aristotle and Aquinas sensation is the basis of generalisation. Forms or general ideas are found *in* things, and are not separate entities directly apprehended by the intellect. In his emphasis on the perception of material objects Aquinas prepared the way for a return from Platonic metaphysical speculation to scientific observation, and supported the theory of knowledge which affirms that " there is nothing in the mind which was not first in the senses ".

His doctrine of the soul was also Aristotelian. Aristotle did not regard the soul as the essence of the man, as though the body were irrelevant. The mind was the form or function, or mode of existence of the body. Soul is sum of the body's powers and processes. A man is not a man at all without his body—or without his mind. Soul and body are therefore together one substance and inseparable.

All this Aquinas accepted. But he added, as some think a little inconsistently, that there is a gradation in the way which form dominates matter. The human soul is a form which dominates matter to such an extent that it possesses in thinking an activity of its own, intrinsically independent of matter. Upon this foundation rests the truth of personal immortality.

Finally Aquinas faced the most searching question of the Middle Ages, the relation of *faith* to *reason*. Siger of Brabant had argued that the Church might be right theologically but wrong scientifically; so that while we are being scientific we need not be concerned whether our conclusions support religion; and when we are being religious we need not expect that our beliefs should harmonise with our scientific beliefs. Aquinas strongly opposed this view and argued that *faith* and *reason* cannot contradict one another. Truth is approached along two paths, that of religion and that of the study of nature. These are two distinct, autonomous and separate spheres, but they can ultimately reach harmony. He held that religion was rational and that reason was divine, therefore all knowledge and all truth are capable of harmonious adjustment.

Aquinas also held, as many theologians did not, that the existence of God could be proved by reason. He admitted, however, that the proof was too difficult for ordinary minds to understand, so that in fact most people accepted it on authority or by faith. He also held that many truths, quite inaccessible to reason, were revealed by God through the Church ; but that these truths were rational in form.

Not all Christian thinkers accepted this position. " There is no merit in a faith whereof human reason furnishes the proof," said one of them. To accept the doctrines of the Church because they were rational seemed to many theologians hardly less offensive than to reject them as irrational.

ST. THOMAS AND ST. DOMINIC

The immense influence and authority of the Thomist philosophy, as it came to be called, owed much to the organisation of the Dominican Order and to its founder *St. Dominic*. Unlike the Franciscans, the Dominicans were, and are, a great teaching order, and they did much to imbue the Church with the new philosophy, which became a powerful ideological support of the Catholic hierarchy.

This is set before the mind and the eye with great dramatic force in the great Dominican Church of Santa Maria Novella in Florence. Here in the Spanish Chapel is set forth in huge frescoes a complete representation of Catholic theology, and of her great instrument of orthodoxy, the Dominican Order.

Below the figures of Our Lady and the Apostles, among them Peter, the rock on which the Church was founded, are depicted all the Virtues, and under these St. Thomas is enthroned holding an open book before him, around him are apostles, saints and patriarchs, and under his feet the great heretics. Below are symbolical figures of the arts and sciences which proceed from and flourish under his theology.

The whole vast composition represents the theology, the civilisation and intellectual culture which derives from and is dependent upon these scenes.

The practical and political way of life flowing from and supported by their theology is depicted on the right wall. Here we see the Duomo of Florence and before it are enthroned the Pope and the Emperor, the spiritual and temporal authorities, and around them the great officers of the Church, monks, friars and nuns, on the one side, and the secular officers, kings, princes, dukes, lawyers and the world at large, on the other. At the feet of the Pope and Emperor we see the sheep, the faithful people, guarded by dogs, spotted black and white—*the Domini canes*—of the Dominican Order.

The great controversy continued through the last years of the Middle Ages; and faith and reason drew more and more apart. *Duns Scotus* (1265–1308) and *William of Ockham* (died 1349) finally separated the two spheres, which had been so sharply distinguished by Aquinas. This was inevitable because, in their view, the harmony expected by Aquinas was not in fact achieved. Ockham denied that any of the central beliefs of religion could be logically demonstrated. Duns Scotus insisted that reason related solely to the realm of the worldly and perceptible. Belief is based on the acceptance of authority.

These views, while put forward in defence of faith, actually prepared the way for the coming rupture of the alliance between philosophy and theology.

This great synthesis which reached its culmination in the thirteenth century, faced the prospect of dissolution in the fourteenth ; and the fifteenth century brought the beginning of the philosophies we still regard as modern.

8

From William of Ockham to Descartes and Francis Bacon

IN 1543 Copernicus, then on his death-bed, received the first printed copy of his work, *De Revolutionibus Orbium Coelestium* (*On the Movements of Heavenly Bodies*). This book marks a turning-point not only in astronomy but in human thought; for the scientific theories of Galileo and Newton, which were developed from the Copernican hypothesis, presented to mankind the picture of the world as a great machine and left the medieval cosmology discredited and unbelievable.

In the later Middle Ages there were, however, trends of thought which prepared the way for this philosophical revolution. One of the most important of these was the rise of *Nominalism*. The controversy between Realists and Nominalists has often seemed of purely academic interest. That is not so; the conflict of theories really reflects two opposite views of the nature of reality which, in turn, has very practical consequences.

Realism,[1] which derived from Plato, held that general ideas, principles and ideals (to put it simply) existed in them-

---

[1] *Realism* does not mean what we might mean by the term today—reference to concrete realities. On the contrary, the *Realism* of the medieval philosopher meant belief in universals as entities having a real existence beyond the world of sense.

selves, in a realm of fixed essences independent of the world of particular things. It is a theory of existent universals. Many important consequences follow from this view. Those who believe in Realism will believe in fixed standards in morals, fixed principles of political organisation, fixed economic law, and, in later times, a clear and definite meaning for such concepts as 'freedom', 'democracy' and other political ideas.

The theory also applies to such corporate entities as the Church, the State, the Trade Guild, and other medieval entities. All these are universals, realities, embodied in actual institutions, as Courage comes down and dwells in a brave man. All brave men belong to the class of the Courageous; all Christians participate in the properties of the class, 'Church', to which they belong. Now the Church is, by definition, that class which is known to be redeemed (just as all vertebrates have backbones, and all men are mortal). Hence the significance of excommunication expelled from the Church, a man no longer has this property, he is therefore damned.

The theory also strongly supported the classification of men into fixed castes, or degrees, such as serfs, freemen, knights, nobles and kings; and also the division of Christians into priests and laymen. A man possesses the characteristics of his kind—its low nature, which cannot be remedied, if he is low, his privileges and powers, which cannot be taken from him, if he is high. It will be noted that these classes are arranged in a hierarchy, from low to high, with increasing authority as one rises from serf and freeman to monarch, or from laymen and priest to Pope. Thus the philosophical (and logical) system reflected a Feudal Order and gave it valuable ideological support.[1]

If the Universal exists *before* the thing, as the Realists

[1] The principal Realists were Erigena, Bernard of Clairvaux and Anselm. Aquinas was a moderate Realist.

believed, then the thing's nature is predetermined and fixed. If the Universal is simply a concept formed by the abstractive activity of thought, and therefore comes into existence *after* the thing, then as things change so must the concept. This is the *Nominalist* point of view, which held that general ideas, principles, and so forth, are only words or names assigned to a number of similar things—that is to say, they have only a logical status. Courage, Fluidity, Democracy, Kingship, do not exist in themselves, they merely reflect human experience, they are the terms we give to this and that.

Nominalism is a sceptical notion. It questions the reality of the main entities and principles dear to medieval thought. These are not realities ; only things experienced are realities. If anything else is held to have existence, and to be deserving of reverence or obedience, we believe that to be so on the basis of faith, and not of reason or experience. Now the principles of medieval thought, religion and social life were held to be such realities. Nominalism said they were either mere names or words, or if they were realities, we knew them to be so only by Revelation.

Nominalism therefore strongly inclined its followers to believe only in concrete experience and what can be inferred from it. As John Stuart Mill was to say, hundreds of years later, " We think by means of concrete phenomena, such as are presented in experience . . . and by means of names, which, being in a peculiar manner associated with certain elements of the concrete images, arrest our attention on these elements."

Clearly Nominalism lay within the scientific tradition, which by the thirteenth century was already beginning to show remarkable signs of vigour. It was congenial to all progress in the direction of establishing a body of knowledge, distinct from theology, and having as its object the natural world. It supported those who in the name of reason separated the natural from the supernatural and preferred to devote their efforts and understanding to the actual world rather than to the transcendental.[1]

Those who imagine that there is nothing but the dust of the past in this controversy should remember that the solution of the most momentous questions to which the human intellect can address itself is inextricably bound up with the solution of this problem. He who has given his answer to it has implicitly constructed his theory of the universe.

This new concern with nature and experience was still further developed by another Franciscan, *William of Ockham (died 1349)*.[2]

The pleasant village of Ockham in Surrey possesses no memorial of its most famous son who was born there and studied at Oxford. He was the greatest of the Nominalists, which meant that he was more interested in particular things than in abstractions and certainly did not regard abstract ideas as existing in themselves ; he was also more interested in particular persons than in corporate entities like the Church and the State and had some hard things to say about ecclesiastical corruption.

With its emphasis on the variety of phenomena and its interests in the affairs of this world the Nominalism of William of Ockham came to be the natural ally of the scientific and the secular point of view. Of even greater significance for the development of science was the instrument of thought which came to be known as Ockham's Razor. This was the principle that entities are not to be multiplied without necessity ; that of all possible explanations, the simplest should be accepted ; that to employ a number of supposed causes or forces when it is possible to use a few is a mistake. This means that if all the facts can be interpreted without assuming some hypothetical entity, there is no ground for assuming it. It calls for the elimination of unnecessary

[1] The principal Nominalists were Rosellinus, Abelard and William of Ockham. [2] Sometimes spelt Occam.

explanatory principles. It was allied to Ockham's Nominalism because it could be used to criticise the Realist habit of treating terms as metaphysical substances and attributing independent existence to Universals.

Ockham's theory of knowledge marks a break with orthodox philosophy. We know in the first place individual things. We do not know essences (i.e. the pure quality of the general class exhibited by the particular, the doggishness of any dog), but the actual objects of sense perception, which may differ as much from one another as individual persons from other persons.

Ockham rejects the notion that we perceive our perceptions. We perceive material objects; there is no intermediary between experience and its object. In this he was already approaching the problem that was to be launched by Locke and Berkeley and to vex the minds of philosophers down to our own time.

In sharp distinction from the belief in the power of reason to grasp material reality was Ockham's denial that any of the central beliefs of religion could be rationally demonstrated. Our concept of God suffers the defects of all concepts of all general ideas, it cannot establish His existence. Logic cannot give us metaphysics.

While Ockham and his fellow Nominalists did believe on authority what they could not accept on rational grounds, others drew different conclusions and began to give up the idea that there were truths we must believe whether they were rational or not. The result was religious scepticism. Another result was the growth of a body of scientific knowledge uncontaminated by religious principles, since, if faith occupied a separate, non-rational compartment, it did not have to be harmonised with the truths of science.

FRANCIS BACON (1561–1626)

Francis Bacon, Lord Chancellor of England under James I, a great lawyer and a brilliant essayist, was the first to put, not so much into clear words as into a startlingly clear example, the concept of progress as it was to dominate the seventeenth, eighteenth and nineteenth centuries. In his last work, *The New Atlantis* (1627), the crew of a ship lost at sea come upon an unknown land where there lives a people in supreme happiness. Their secret proves to be that in their government there are no politicians, but only geologists, biologists, chemists, sociologists, economists and philosophers. Indeed, there is little government at all, for all these are wholly engaged in controlling nature, rather than in ruling men. The principle of this new order was " the knowledge of causes and secret motions of things ; and the enlargement of the bounds of human empire, to the effecting of all things possible "

Even as a student at Cambridge Bacon had revolted against the scholastic philosophy. It did not seem to him fruitful. Scientific advance was doing more for the world. Printing, gunpowder and the compass—these were the forces that were driving and changing human life. Philosophy, as it existed, actually stood in the way of the advancement of learning and of civilisation, and must be swept away with its frivolous disputations, confutations and verbosities.

This degenerate learning did chiefly reign among the schoolmen, who having sharp and strong wits, and abundance of leisure, and small variety of reading (but their wits being shut up in the cells of a few authors, chiefly Aristotle, as their persons were shut up in the cells of monasteries and colleges), and knowing little history, either of nature or time, did, out of no great quantity of matter, and infinite agitation of wit, spin out unto us these laborious webs of learning, which are extant in their books. For the wit and mind of man, if it work upon matter, which is the contemplation of the creatures of God, worketh according to the stuff, and is limited thereby ; but if it work upon itself, as the spider worketh his web, then it is endless, and brings forth indeed cobwebs of learning, admirable for the fineness of thread and work, but of no substance or profit.[1]

Bacon included Plato and Aristotle in his condemnation. Truth was not, as Plato thought, the native inhabitant of the mind, it came from outside, by observation and experiment. "When philosophy is severed from its roots in experience, it becomes a dead thing."

Hence a new philosophy is wanted :

1. "Not an opinion to be held but a work to be done ".
2. Not abstract truth but mastery over nature.
3. Not logical deductions from untested first principles but the interrogation of nature, leading to the changing of the world.

Only when men mean by knowledge the understanding which comes from acting upon nature and changing it will philosophy show us that life is not a vale of tears ; only in so far as we learn *to make Nature do better*.

This new method of reasoning must begin with doubt, with the testing of first principles assumed without investigation, and the rejection of knowledge not verified by experience. But doubt is not for its own sake, not because scepticism is preferred to knowledge. "If a man will begin with certainties, he shall end in doubt ; but if he will be content to begin in doubt he shall end in certainties."

The prevalent scepticism, he says, arose from an intellectualistic approach. To ask theoretically, Can man know

[1] Francis Bacon, *The Advancement of Learning*.

truth ? is to breed scepticism and inaction. Stop debating and begin to work. Seek a practical and historical rather than a speculative answer to the problem of truth. Whether you can know and how much you know will be shown by what you can do.

DESCARTES (1596–1650)

Descartes was as rationalistic as any of the earlier critics of medievalism which we have mentioned, but his approach to the problem of truth was totally different. Rejecting the untested assumptions of scholasticism, he sought the basis of truth and reasoning in absolutely certain and irreducible *ideas*, the ultimate postulates of thought. Bacon had stressed the appeal to facts, but had neglected the rational, explanatory phase of scientific thinking. Descartes emphasised the rational element and overlooked the empirical.[1]

But together Bacon and Descartes were the forerunners of the Enlightenment, that movement which regarded the Middle Ages as a period of darkness from which clear thinking (based on reason or facts) was now at last going to deliver men into the light of truth. They gave expression to a real and widespread desire to shake off the past and to advance in the power of certain new conceptions of nature and man to an unparalleled future. This is eloquently proclaimed in Descartes' *Discourse on Method*.

I perceived it to be possible to arrive at knowledge highly useful in life ; and in room of the speculative philosophy usually taught in the schools, to discover a practical, by means of which, knowing the force and action of fire, water, air, the stars, the heavens, and all the other bodies that surround us, as distinctly as we know the various crafts of our artisans, we might also apply them in the

[1] *Empirical*, based on the observation of facts of experience.

same way to all the uses to which they are adapted, and thus render ourselves the lords and possessors of nature.

Descartes, a member of the lesser French nobility, was educated at a Jesuit college, where he distinguished himself in mathematics. But turning in a spirit of weariness from the aridity of medieval thought, he entirely abandoned the study of letters, and, as he tells us in his *Discourse on Method*, " resolved no longer to seek any other science than the knowledge of myself or of the great book of the world. I spent the remainder of my youth in travelling, in visiting courts and armies, in holding intercourse with men of different dispositions and ranks."

He settled in Holland in 1628, where he might expect less interference from ecclesiastical authority than in France. Always a little nervous in the face of such disapproval, he withdrew his book *Le Monde* after the condemnation of Galileo in 1633.

After the publication of his two most important books, the *Discourse on Method* and *Meditations on the First Philosophy*, his fame spread among educated people throughout Europe. He became the philosophic friend of Princess Elizabeth, daughter of Frederick V, Elector Palatine, and was eventually summoned to the court of Queen Christina of Sweden to instruct her in philosophy. The Queen, however, required his presence at five o'clock in the morning and Descartes was accustomed to lie in bed thinking until midday. This ordeal and the winter cold were too much for him and he died the next year, in 1650.

DESCARTES' DISCOURSE ON METHOD AND
    MEDITATIONS

Descartes saw that in philosophy, as it was then accepted, endless disputations prevailed and generally agreed truth was never reached. In mathematics, on the other hand, all were compelled to the same indubitable conclusions. Why is this? Firstly, he argued, it was due to proceeding from untested assumptions. Let us then clear the mind, by systematic doubt, of all presuppositions and retain only those clear and distinct ideas which are indubitable. This was not the empirical method of basing everything on experience, it was the rationalist method of arguing logically from " atoms of obviousness and intelligibility ", as his clear ideas have been called. Unfortunately, while these seemed quite certain to Descartes, thinkers have been arguing about them ever since, which is perhaps why Descartes is called ' the father of philosophy '.

Descartes, then, starts from these innate ideas. What are they? He points out that whatever we doubt we cannot doubt that we are there doubting, and to doubt is to think. Therefore *cogito ergo sum*, ' I think therefore I am '. This, then, is a clear and distinct idea, and is indubitable. We must also believe in the axioms of geometry, and that everything has a cause, and so on. Now thinking is the act of pure mind, it is not dependent on any material thing, therefore " I am a substance whose whole essence consists only in thinking ", this also is obvious. But there is also a material world which does not think, but whose property it is to exist in space. Thus there are two completely different basic substances : Mind which does not occupy space, whose sole property is to think ; and matter, which does not think, but is extended (spatial) substance.

Finally, on the grounds that the idea of *existence* is inseparable from the idea of a perfect being, he believed in God (an argument that has not commended itself to most philosophers).

God was necessary for Descartes in order that he might assure himself of the existence of the material world. Ideas are mental ; but while they seem to *represent* physical objects, how do we know that they do ? Clearly mind, being pure thought, cannot make contact and handle material objects.

It can only look at mental pictures of them in the dark chamber of the mind. But if God exists and is perfect He would not deceive us, and so we may believe that a physical universe corresponding to our mental picture actually exists.

This problem inevitably arises because of the radical dualism of Descartes' philosophy. He had split the world into two distinct substances, which were absolutely incapable of interacting. Mind cannot either know or handle or affect matter; and matter cannot impress itself upon, or affect, mind. How, then, can we *know* material things? This was no problem to Aquinas and Aristotle because for them mind was the form or activity of the body and not a separate substance, but this distinction of mind and matter has haunted Western philosophy ever since the time of Descartes. Professor Ryle calls it the fallacy of ' the ghost in the machine '; an error of thinking that we must get rid of, he thinks,—a totally unnecessary dilemma springing from the erroneous assumptions of Descartes.[1]

DESCARTES' CONTRIBUTION TO PHILOSOPHY AND SCIENCE

The work of Descartes is to be evaluated not so much in relation to metaphysical speculation, which he seems to have put on the wrong tack, as to the development of science. Galileo had declared that philosophy was written " in that vast book which stands ever open before our eyes—the universe; but it cannot be read until we have learnt its language and become familiar with the characters in which it is written. It is written in the language of mathematics." In other words, *the truth of nature consists in mathematical facts.* If that is so, what is real and intelligible in nature is what is measurable and quantitative; therefore to get at material reality we have to free thought from sensation, for sensation

[1] For a further discussion of Professor Ryle's view see Chapter 15.

gives us colour and sound, which are not quantitative, not measurable. It is only their colourless, soundless physical causes which are measurable, and therefore they alone are real. Only when we reduce phenomena to mathematical terms are they (*a*) perfectly rational, (*b*) completely real. This is nature at bottom.

There was something more, later to be demonstrated by Sir Isaac Newton. Nature does not only consist of separate facts describable in mathematical terms. It is a *system*. The whole of nature is actually, concretely, geometrical. It is coordinated in its parts, so that one part can be deduced from the others, and it possesses no characteristics that are not so deducible.

It is only by thus excluding everything qualitative and reducing everything to the measurable and systematic that nature becomes an object of knowledge. This has been the view of many thinkers since Descartes. James Clark Maxwell affirms that " the aim of exact sciences is to reduce the problems of nature to the determinations of quantities by operations with numbers ".

DESCARTES AND THE SOUL

This view of nature strips the world of its qualities, of its colour and sound, and, of course, of mind and life as something interacting with the physical. It reduces the world to a machine. Its changes and processes are produced and directed by antecedent causes, just as the movement of a billiard ball *follows* the impact of the cue. But in the world of thought quite different causes operate, we do certain things because we envisage a distant end ; we are pulled by *what is not yet*. Before Galileo and Descartes, men thought that nature was the scene of a somewhat similar *purposeful* causation, something was *intending* a particular effect, things were moving towards a distant, as yet unrealised, goal. Now Descartes substituted for this conception purely mathematical and mechanical explanations (efficient causes), totally abandoning occult influences, or ' tendencies ' in this or that direction (final causes). No explanation by final causes is received in the science of nature ; for mathematics admits only mechanical relations of cause and effect.

Descartes could not possibly have established this theory had he not at the same time found a place in which to put everything he had extruded from the physical universe— qualities (i.e. colour and other sensed properties of things), minds and human purposes. Minds form a class of beings outside nature, and all qualities (colour and so forth) are appearances and only found in minds. Sound consists in reality of physical vibrations, what we *hear* as sounds are mental events. Colours, sound, smell, hot and cold are in the mind. *We* feel heat, not the fire, which is only molecules in movement.

This was the most radical and influential revolution in the history of thought from Aristotle to Kant. It gave the ' all clear ' to physical science and provided a philosophical framework, a world view, which explained and justified the Newtonian, mechanical cosmology. It assured men that nature was lawful and therefore completely subject to control. Descartes even extended this mechanistic idea to the human body, making it an automation, containing a soul, but in itself a machine.

This was his achievement, but it carried with it a legacy of philosophical conundrums that were to vex philosophy for over three hundred years, and are by no means disposed of even yet.

9

Spinoza

SPINOZA (1623–77)

SPINOZA was born a Jew but was excommunicated. His family had come to Holland from Spain to escape the Inquisition. Here he lived simply earning his living by grinding lenses.

In his thirty-third year he completed his great work of philosophy called the *Ethics*, written in Latin in scholastic terms and in the form of a series of mathematical demonstrations, with axioms, definitions, theorems and proofs, to exclude with the hardness of glass any emotional impulses or other confusions which might creep into his thinking.

Spinoza had a strange reputation. He has been called ' a God-intoxicated man ', that is a man obsessed with God, a pantheist who saw God in everything ; but he was also seen as a materialist and a determinist, an extreme rationalist denying at every point both the supernatural, as religious men knew it, and human freedom.

GOD AND NATURE

Spinoza had a two-fold conception of the Universe, firstly as *natura naturans*, that is to say nature begetting, nature as the source, as infinite potentiality, the whole, transcendent and ineffable ; secondly as *natura naturata*, nature as the infinity of worlds and objects and events into which the

whole divides itself and in which the One displays the
potentialities latent within it.

MIND AND MATTER

Spinoza saw the world not as a dualism but as one universal
substance, infinite and eternal, but possessing two aspects or
attributes (known to man), *extension* and *thought*. Thus God
or Nature is from one aspect material, and from the other
spiritual. Now this is true not only of the whole but of
every part. Every sensation is the mental aspect of a bodily
condition. There is one process, seen now inwardly as
thought, and now outwardly as motion. There is but one
entity, seen now inwardly as mind, now outwardly as matter.

When we apply this to the problem of the interaction of
mind and body we see that our will and a bodily movement
are not cause and effect, but two aspects of one and the
same concrete event. There is a discernible cause-and-effect
sequence within the mental series and within the physical
series, but not action by mind on matter, or *vice versa*.

THE MODES OF THE DIVINE BEING

If mind and matter are attributes of Being, this ultimate
Reality appears in various *modes*. A mode is any individual
thing or event which Reality transiently assumes. Modes
are fashions of the eternal Reality, and belong, of course, to
natura naturata. Man is such a mode. His physical being
is a particular expression of God's extension, of God as
material; his thinking an expression of God's thought.

But since Man is a mode of Being he cannot be separated
from Nature (God). He is a part of Nature, through and
through. Men are not cut off from the things of this world.
They are physically and spiritually members of the realm of
nature. If dogs and horses are brutes that perish, man is
a brute that perishes. If dogs and horses are biological
mechanisms, so is man. Conversely, if man is not only

material but also thinks, dogs and horses are not only material but have their spiritual aspect too. If there is something eternal about man, there is something eternal about horses and dogs. Man is utterly and completely, without reservation of any kind, of a piece with the rest of nature.

GOD

God is the cause of all things, but not a cause *outside* what he creates, but *inside*. He is the immanent cause of all things. God is the causal chain or process, the law and structure of the world. God is not personal; He is a vast impersonal Being coterminous with the Universe. The mind of God is all the mentality that is scattered over space and time, the diffused consciousness that animates the world.

We are in error in demanding a God like ourselves to see all things, to hear our prayers, to will and act like an exalted man.

> I believe that a triangle, if only it had power of speech, would say that God is eminently triangular, and a circle would say that the Divine Nature is eminently circular, and in this way each thing would ascribe its own attributes to God.[1]

NECESSITY

Freedom, in the usual sense, is a complete illusion. " From the infinite nature of God all things follow by the same necessity, and in the same way, as it follows from the nature of a triangle that its three angles are equal to two right angles." [2]

The Universe is what it is not because of any plan or Divine intention, but because all things follow in this way from its essential nature. There are no willed ends; everywhere and in all things strict and inexorable causality reigns.

[1] Spinoza, *Letters*.   [2] Spinoza, *Ethics*.

If we think we are experiencing freedom this is only the result of a direct perception of the effect being combined with ignorance of the cause. No doubt a stone flying through the air would think it was free.

True freedom comes not from ignorance or from independence of determining forces, but from knowledge, from the realisation that we have no interests or possibilities of our own apart from the whole of which we form a part.

ETHICS[1]

Aristotle taught that every ideal has a natural basis, that is to say, there must be something in the world which is made to manifest or to grow into that ideal; and every natural thing therefore has its ideal fulfilment. Spinoza also taught that every natural thing, including man, strives to realise its proper form. The essence of anything lies in its self-preservation, in *the endeavour to persist in its own being*. Virtue is this maintenance of one's being, and this implies the power to do so. We *must and do* possess the power to be what we essentially are. Happiness is the exercise of this power. The more a man can preserve his being and seek what is useful to him, the greater is his virtue, and his happiness.

What, then, is the good? That which enhances man's existence. " Men do not desire something because it is good, but they call it good because they desire it." [2] The basic motive is the desire to live well now, to lead a well-rounded, happy life. Happiness is the goal of conduct, and it comes from the pleasure we enjoy in passing from a lesser state of completeness or fulfilment to a greater. And " No one ever neglects anything which he judges to be good, except with the hope of gaining a greater good."

Spinoza builds his ethic on inevitable and justifiable

[1] Spinoza's *Ethics* includes his whole metaphysical system. Part IV contains his ethical propositions.   [2] Spinoza, *Ethics*.

egoism or self-realisation. Life's whole purpose is to acquire an adequate idea of oneself. To achieve this man must identify his own activity with that of the all-pervading essence, and discard those emotions in whose grip, however active he may have thought himself, he was only the plaything of unreal forces.

Man becomes the adequate cause of his own actions, and therefore and in that sense free, when the good he seeks is no longer determined by a limited vision and the immediate feelings belonging to it, but is a good common to all rational natures.

SPINOZA'S ACHIEVEMENT

Spinoza lived in a time of transition between two epochs —the dark, ascetic medieval period, which had crushed individuality, was beginning to retreat into the past, and the new era of human history which was to reveal a new intellectual horizon and expand the life of man in every field, material and spiritual. His great contribution was not appreciated in his lifetime. It was not, indeed, until Hegel appeared that the significance of his philosophy became apparent, both in its strength and weakness.

Spinoza saw the Universe as essentially unchanging, whereas in fact it is in constant development; therefore he does not take time or history seriously. It is difficult today for us to recapture the state of mind in which the universe is conceived as essentially a static system.

But he overcame the hopeless dualism of Descartes by embracing both mental and physical events in one substance. Substance itself he sees to be not dead matter or pure spirit, but has body and has mind. Since he is unable to comprehend the emergence of new qualities in an evolutionary way, this double aspect theory leads him to attribute a mental life to inorganic matter. Later naturalistic philosophers are content to find a mental aspect only in animals with brains.

Spinoza never freed his materialism from a certain theological envelope which he absorbed from his religious tradition. He sees the entire Universe as a living, not a dead, mechanism, for the order of things is the order of perfect goodness and wisdom, and is continuously sustained by the intense consciousness of God. Spinoza thus gave naturalistic answers, to the extent possible in the intellectual climate of the time, excluding all supernatural or mystical explanations, to the problems confronting the philosophy of his age.

In ethics Spinoza, like Aristotle, does not seek for moral principles outside man and good in themselves. Every man should seek what is truly useful to him ; but that in the long run is knowledge, perfect understanding. Blessedness is that contentment of Spirit which arises from knowledge of God (i.e. of Reality).

Spinoza goes on to say that since men necessarily seek their own preservation and the indefinite extension of their power and liberty this must be the starting-point of an inquiry into society and politics. Social organisation comes into being because in perfecting his being nothing is more useful to man than man. *Man is a God to man.* " My own power increases with every step towards cooperation that joins it to the power of other men."

Spinoza believed that political consent and obedience could only be justified as rational self-interest ; and this would be so when it could be shown to be the acceptance of the lesser of two evils. It is a deprivation, it is submission, but it is better than anarchy and insecurity. Spinoza does not base political authority on the acceptance of Divine Right in monarchs or magistrates, but solely on social utility. Appeals to ultimate moral notions or to supernatural sanctions seemed to him a superstitious or dishonest playing with words. The justification of any moral or political decision, therefore, must always be to show that the decision makes for safety and happiness, either immediately or in the long run. This point of view was so thoroughly secular and naturalistic that it seemed to his contemporaries, still immersed to a considerable extent in the ideology of a feudal society, dangerous and heretical. The true appreciation of Spinoza both as a metaphysician and a moralist was not to come for over two hundred years.

10

Leibniz

LEIBNIZ (1646–1716)

IT appears to be widely held in academic circles today
that philosophers should not be expected to show any
interest in public affairs, problems of conduct, or even the
meaning of life. If they have any views on these affairs
they are supposed to keep them to themselves, and to disavow
any connection between them and their philosophical beliefs.
As we shall see, Whitehead, who was a severe critic of
empiricism and its anti-metaphysical tendency, has a very
definite philosophy of life, but he appears to be the last of
the great system builders and his successors are for the most
part negative and critical in their approach to philosophy.

If this is the case today, it was certainly not always so.
Socrates argued in the market-place about every conceivable
topic, moral, political and religious. Aristotle was the tutor
of Alexander the Great and as a mature philosopher was as
interested in statecraft as he was in metaphysics. Augustine
formulated a theory on the relation of the Church and secular
society which governed their relationship for centuries.
Aquinas taught that state authority was God-given and his
followers asserted the Church had a definite authority over
secular rulers should they contravene the Will of God.
Descartes spent much of his time in courts and armies and
was the guide and mentor of princes. Spinoza wrote two
political works, the *Theological-Political Treatise* and the

Political Treatise. Hegel's whole life work culminated in his exposition of the State as the ground of human freedom and the culmination of rational order in the world. Locke and Hobbes were active politicians, their influence arising wholly from their views, so were Bentham and Mill. Bosanquet in our time wrote *The Philosophical Theory of the State*. But after that, " the rest is silence ".

Now if ever there was a philosopher who was passionately concerned and deeply involved in public affairs and whose whole philosophy was a guide to political action it was Gottfried Wilhelm Leibniz, born at Leipzig on 21st June, 1646, two years before the end of the Thirty Years War. He could read Latin at 12 and entered the University as a Law student at 15, took a doctor's degree in 1666 and entered the service of the Elector of Mainz to revise the Statute Book of that principality. He did far more than this for his master and was soon deeply involved in politics. He advocated a Union of Rhineland States in view of French threats and eventually a League of Christian States which, he suggested, should fight the Mohammedans instead of one another, and indicated the conquest of Egypt as a likely prize (a hint that was subsequently taken by Napoleon). In Paris he met the Cartesian philosophers and their critics, and many leaders of scientific thought, with whom he discussed mathematics, mechanics, optics, hydrostatics and his famous philosophical theory of *monads*. He was a great mathematician and discovered the Differential and Integral Calculus and invented a calculating machine. He visited London where he met Newton, Boyle and others. At The Hague he met Spinoza and was profoundly influenced by him—but in a critical direction. This bare summary of his energetic life and wide erudition can barely suggest the range of his interests and the power of his intellect.

If one wanted a key thought to indicate what was behind both his political activity and his philosophy it could be suggested that he was essentially the philosopher of *reconciliation*. Metaphysics are a technical expression of the social outlook of an age,[1] and undoubtedly the world of Leibniz called aloud for someone to reconcile its conflicting interests, national rivalries and warring doctrines.

Leibniz tried to combine the rationalism of Spinoza and the supernaturalism of the Church, determinism and a Providential Order, materialism and idealism. This desire to reconcile antagonistic forces and achieve unity is reflected in one of his most important theories—that of *Pre-established Harmony*.

The philosophy of Leibniz comprises two closely related doctrines :

1. The theory of the individuality of the monads.
2. The law of Pre-established Harmony.

1. THE DOCTRINE OF THE MONADS

Leibniz had studied both Descartes and Spinoza but, while he fully accepted their determination to make reality rational and intelligible through and through, there were features of their system which he disliked. Descartes reduced everything to smooth, undifferentiated matter performing different kinds of motion ; Spinoza saw the material world and the spiritual world as modifications of one substance. Leibniz did not like this all-embracing identity, the swallowing up of particulars in *one* substance. He was an intense individualist in an age in which individualism was growing. Bankers and merchants were vying with aristocrats and princes in the determination to run the world, intellectuals were asserting their independence, and Reason was making a special appeal to men to think for themselves. Leibniz responded to the spirit of the time and came to see the universe as an aggregate of *individuals*. These he called monads. His theory was a

[1] Lodge, *The Great Thinkers.*

metaphysical projection of social life as Leibniz observed it in the seventeenth century, with each individual conscious mainly of himself and his wants, and a little deficient in genuine appreciation of his neighbours.

Before we explain the nature of these monads more precisely there is another difference from his great predecessors which we have to examine. Leibniz did not at all like the radical *dualism* of Descartes who had postulated *two* ultimate substances—mind and matter, which were by definition completely incapable of interaction ; nor was he prepared to accept Spinoza's idea of persons as modes or parts of One Substance, a theory which did less than justice to the individual.

For Spinoza's *One* he substituted the *Many* ; for the block universe he substituted *atomism*. Ultimate reality is an assemblage of non-spatial minds, spirit-atoms, centres of force, each capable of self-activity and *self-subsistence*. The idea of self-subsistence is important. It is for classical philosophy a property only of God, for everything else, including the person, is dependent and not self-subsistent. For Leibniz every monad is self-subsistent.

These monads are all alive and all perceive, but they are of three kinds. *Bare monads* who perceive confusedly as if in sleep (the nearest Leibniz would get to matter), *souls*, as in animals, and reasoning souls, as in men, which we can call *spirits*. (As we ascend this hierarchy the motive force becomes first instinct and later will. Thought and will together produce freedom and therefore happiness.) At each level the area and intensity of perception increases, so that at the level of mind there is a clear apprehension of logical concepts leading to a metaphysical view of experience. Above even this level is the Monad of monads, God, the master mind who adjusts the others to one another and is responsible for the harmony of the whole.

2. THE PRE-ESTABLISHED HARMONY

Now it is important to understand that every monad is quite independent, so much so that it is shut off from every other monad. The monad 'has no windows'; yet each monad mirrors the Universe, because God had given it a nature which spontaneously reveals to it what is outside itself.

Leibniz solves the problem of how mind interacts with body in a similar way. The mind is a monad without doors and windows, the body is also a collection of atoms or monads. If one seems to affect the other it is because there is a predetermined sequence of events, one bodily and one mental which run parallel, just as two clocks strike at the same moment because they are wound up to do so. This is the theory of psycho-physical parallelism and it is designed to overcome the theory of interaction between body and mind. The two series run in parallel because God has so constructed the monads. There is between them a pre-established harmony. Thus when a man raises his gun to shoot a bird flying overhead, the mental sequence of seeing and willing and controlling the arm does not affect the body and the pulling of the trigger, the two series run independently but together, so that it *seems* that mind is controlling matter. To those who thought this pre-established harmony very queer, Leibniz pointed out what admirable evidence it afforded for the existence of God!

There is another and wider aspect of the pre-established harmony. The whole world consists of these graded monads, some in a low position, some more exalted; great masses of humanity always in the position of 'animal souls', requiring and receiving direction from the higher ups, and a special position, just under God, for 'minds', i.e. for intellectuals like Leibniz, who cooperate with God in adjusting lower monads to one another so as to bring out the best that is in them.

This theory is clearly the work of a trained administrator, confident in his ability to combine, organise, harmonise, reconcile and make the best out of his material. At the bottom we find individuals who, like the bare monads, are practically identical. At the top the master-organiser responsible for the pre-established harmony ; in between the different grades of rulers and administrators. It reminds us instantly of the feudal hierarchy of Thomas Aquinas and of Plato's men of Iron, Brass, Silver, ruled by the men of Gold, the philosopher kings. The difference from St. Thomas is that his system rested on Revelation and Authority while that of Leibniz rested on Reason.

THE BEST OF ALL POSSIBLE WORLDS

Hardly more fantastic than the theory of monads and their harmonious organisation was Leibniz's conclusion that the world thus controlled must be the best world which reason can conceive. Even pain and sin are only means to a good end, though from the standpoint of the individual that is far from plain, and the world may appear to be very far from perfect.

Leibniz is convinced that God, the ideally skilful administrator, can so control everything and everyone, that while preserving the independent way of life of each, they will work together to make the best of all possible worlds, i.e. that system in which the greatest possible quantity and quality of value is realised. In consequence this actual world, with its wars and brutalities and suffering, with its privileged classes and unjust and tyrannical rulers, with its stupidities and ignorance, is the best world which an Infinite Intelligence could devise and, in His Infinite Goodness, bring into existence.

Voltaire poured scorn on this complacent optimism concerning this best of all possible worlds, with everything in it a necessary evil, and, in his novel *Candide*, told the story of a prince who insisted on believing in the best side of everything in spite of the most disconcerting appearances, always persuaded that all was for the best by the famous Dr. Pangloss.

We must do Leibniz the justice, however, to point out that all he meant was that a world in which certain evils were, shall we say, forcibly removed, would necessarily develop other evils and so turn out to be a worse one; on the other hand, some great goods may be found to be logically bound up with certain evils. It was not the best *conceivable* world, it was the best that was *possible* to have, taking all things into consideration.

However, it does seem to argue that whatever *is*, is right, and it is a philosophy that is far easier to accept if you happen to be at the top of the social scale than if you are at the bottom. As Bertrand Russell says, " This argument apparently satisfied the Queen of Prussia. Her serfs continued to suffer evil, while she continued to enjoy the good, and it was comforting to be assured by a great philosopher that this was just and right " (*History of Western Philosophy*).

LEIBNIZ AND THE INDIVIDUAL

From the seventeenth century onwards philosophy discovers and enhances the value and independence of the individual; to this the Protestant Reformation on the one hand, and the Italian Renaissance on the other, contributed in the fifteenth and sixteenth centuries not a little. But it is in Leibniz that the individual for the first time becomes the absolute centre of philosophic thought.

Let us go back to the soul as a monad. We have here the view that the individual notion of each person involves once and for all everything that will ever happen to him. But God has so implanted the predetermined sequence of events in the life of every individual that each, while carefully preserving its especial and independent way of living and experiencing, works together with all the others to achieve perfect social harmony. This is immensely superior, from the individualist standpoint, to the theory of Spinoza which rooted the individual in the Whole, in which he was but a surface ripple, a mere modification, something not existing in its own right at all. Leibniz leaves a place for me and my ambition. I have precisely my own self, interfered with by no one else, and not interfering with the intimate life of anyone else. True, the life-history of each of us is pre-determined, but this is after all autonomy. I am ruled by what *I* am and am free from outward constraint. That is real freedom. Thought is free, not subject to external control. Each thinks and plans for himself as he wills. We plan and reason for ourselves. Each lives his own life, fully and freely, making his own contribution to reality.

And reality needs our different contributions. Each monad is a living mirror of the whole, but each represents the universe in a unique way. The whole needs every separated, unique part, and needs each person to play out his particular role. But it is not our responsibility to see to it that our separate instruments combine with all the others. We play them each in a soundproof room. It is God, the great Conductor, who is responsible for the ultimate harmony. All that we have to do is to express ourselves in our uniqueness, and He will see to the rest.

Leibniz seems to have believed that the power of any soul to understand and perceive developed gradually. We ourselves may at the beginning have the limited range of simple monads. "Then, as on waking from a state of stupor, we become conscious of our perception." The range and depth of our thinking increases, we have memory and general ideas. There is philosophic reflection upon the self, upon experience ; the formation of an ideal self, an ideal world. This is rather similar to Plato's men in the cave, who begin by looking at shadows, but are at last brought out to see things as they are and to face the light. This idea proved stimulating to the literary men of Germany. The view of the individual as unfolding his personality in a cosmic setting, the whole being linked and woven together into purpose and unity, found expression in German literature up to Goethe and Schiller. Lessing, in particular, was struck, on reading Leibniz, with the idea of the struggle of the individual soul up from the dark depths of the unconscious to the clear light of the conscious. From this time interest in German literature centred upon the individual, his hopes, ideals, feelings, struggles, defeats and victories. It became the vital force of the romantic movement.

THE SIGNIFICANCE OF LEIBNIZ

1. Leibniz was an idealist ; that is to say the ultimate substance was not matter, or, as for Descartes, matter and mind, or a combination of these as aspects of one substance. *The ultimate reality consists of minds.* Matter for him was something other than extension, it was something like a swarm of monads, looking like a solid structure, but resolving itself into individuals on closer inspection.

2. Leibniz recognised levels of organisation in nature, which was organic, that is to say composed of living elements making up larger living wholes—atoms forming molecules, molecules cells, cells organisms, and organisms forming societies. The final unity is the universe itself, controlled by the supreme Monad. Now we shall find something remarkably like this when we come to the contemporary philosopher Whitehead ; it is a conception of profound importance.

When the microscope revealed to man the hitherto invisible swarming life of pond water, it looked like a vindication of the theories of Leibniz. When further study revealed bacterial life existing even on very small organisms, this offered further confirmation. Men accepted the fact that there was nothing sterile, nothing dead in the universe. In every particle they believed a world composed of an infinity of creatures to exist.

3. Leibniz was a Pluralist, not a Monist. He rejected Spinoza's account of the Universe as ultimately One. As Russell says, if we were taking an inventory of the universe, Leibniz's total would be a very large number, and Spinoza's one. This notion has been taken up repeatedly by philosophers who are opposed to Monism, whether materialist or idealist, notably by Bertrand Russell and William James.

4. *Leibniz believed in Innate Ideas*. Every monad has enfolded within it all the ideas which will emerge in the course of its development, because it has no windows to see out of and no information can get into it. This was a view which was to be radically opposed by John Locke.

11

Locke and Berkeley

DESCARTES, Spinoza and Leibniz were all *rationalists*, that is to say, they believed that the unaided reason can itself discover certain basic truths, and, building logically upon them, erect a complete system of metaphysics. They believed that they could enunciate the set of principles which define the universal form of reality and which make the world intelligible. For Descartes these principles were his ' clear and distinct ideas ', for Leibniz they were certain innate ideas implanted by God in the mind of every soul. Working with these principles, they believed it should be possible to arrive at a system of knowledge in which the world is known as a totality, its parts interlocking, its behaviour regular and dependable. Spinoza went even further and declared that " the order and connection of ideas is the same as the order and connection of things ", that a perfectly rational system of ideas *is* the order of nature ; it is both fact and theoretical system.

The upshot of rationalism was that everything was necessary, logically deducible from first principles. Everything was part of a perfect rational system. Facts *must* fit into the perfect scheme. There are therefore no contingent facts, no brute facts, no facts that are just inexplicably but indubitably *there*, like the greenness of grass, which might just as well have been red.

Now this whole mode of thought bears a close relationship

to the Realism of Plato and the medieval philosophers, which had been opposed by the Nominalists, who discovered their principles and general ideas not by rational intuition, but proceeded *inductively* [1] from the facts of experience. This scholastic debate came to an end with William of Ockham in the fourteenth century. But three hundred years later the empiricist philosophers of the seventeenth century launched a somewhat similar attack on Rationalism. These philosophers are Bacon, Hobbes, Locke, Berkeley and Hume, and later William James.

Locke (1632–1704) believed (with Aquinas) that there was nothing in the mind that was not first in the senses, and therefore that there were *no innate ideas*. There is no knowledge *in advance* of experience (*a priori*), but only *after* experience (*a posteriori*). Knowledge is simply ordered experience. This being so there are definite *limits to the human understanding*. This is indeed the theme of his most important book, the *Essay Concerning Human Understanding*. How he came to write it is interesting. He tells us that in the winter of 1670 five or six friends met in his room to discuss questions of morality and religion. They quickly found themselves at a standstill by the difficulties that arose on every side. Locke proposed that before engaging in their discussions they should give consideration to the necessary limits of their understanding. He jotted down the headings of this proposed inquiry for the next meeting. What was thus begun almost by chance was continued by him for twenty years, and appeared in 1690. Thus was launched a philosophical treatise which was to play an all-important part in the intellectual development of Europe, in that Enlightenment which represented the movement of critical thought against tradition, authority and all untested assumptions.

[1] *Induction :* Proceeding to general assertions on the basis of a number of observed particular facts.

LOCKE THE MAN

Locke was an Oxford scholar and a physician. He was a protestant and a political liberal.[1] He fled the country in the time of James II, who was Catholic in faith and autocratic in politics. When James was deposed Locke returned to England and served as a Colonial Secretary, helping to draft the constitution of the State of Carolina. Locke was a widely read man, met everyone of intellectual importance and carried on a voluminous correspondence.[2] He formulated the philosophy of the men who had overthrown the Stuarts and were building constitutional government in England,[3] and wrote tracts on *Toleration* and on *Education*.

In 1691 he returned to the country residence of Sir Francis and Lady Masham at Oates in Essex ; his distinguished friend the Earl of Shaftesbury left him a pension and here he stayed until his death.

THE LIMITS OF THE UNDERSTANDING

The philosophy of Locke, unlike that of Spinoza and the great German philosophers, does not make difficult reading. All the great empiricists wrote well and clearly. His thesis is a simple one : he is critical of ambitious cosmic speculations ; he rejects tradition and authority and all untested assumptions ; he rejects innate ideas ; he is opposed to rationalism as a philosophy, that is to say to knowledge obtained by the use of principles given with the mind, independently of experience, and constituting in themselves the faculty of reason.

Locke believed, on the contrary, that all knowledge was

[1] The term at that time was Whig.
[2] In the Bodleian Library in Oxford are some 2,550 letters sent to him by various correspondents.
[3] He wrote an important *Treatise of Civil Government*. His political theories are discussed in C. L. Wayper's *Political Thought* (Teach Yourself Books).

derived from sense experience. The mind apart from sense experience has no other means of knowing any kind of truth. Sense experience is the result of the impact of matter on the sense organs. However widely the mind roams or however high our speculations soar, sense experience is the origin and is the sole test of their validity.

All these sublime thoughts which tower above the clouds, and reach as high as heaven itself, take their rise and footing here; in all that great extent wherein the mind wanders in these remote speculations it may seem to be elevated with, it stirs not one jot beyond these ideas which sense or reflection have offered for its contemplation.

The result of such views was devastating. They wrought havoc with philosophical speculation, with elaborate metaphysical systems reared on untested assumptions, and on principles accepted by intuition or regarded as implanted in the mind (innate ideas). They were equally critical of every kind of intuitionism [1] and mysticism.

Locke's theory was an attack on credulity, on uncritical thinking, on believing more than we are entitled to. The unerring mark of love of truth, says Locke, is " not entertaining any proposition with greater assurance than the proofs it is built on will warrant ".

The significance of Locke's views was not only philosophical. It undermined ecclesiastical and political authority which in turn was the basis of institutions which Locke and the Whigs wanted to get rid of (such as the Divine Right of Kings, for instance). Locke rejected all moral and political principles which could not be shown to arise out of sense experience. Bertrand Russell says, " Only those who have allowed themselves to be affected by the scholastics will

[1] *Intuitionism :* Any philosophy in which intuition is appealed to as the basis of knowledge. *Intuition :* The direct and immediate apprehension of rational truths, or spiritual beings, or other minds, etc.

realise how much metaphysical lumber this method of thinking sweeps away."

Locke was strongly opposed to all religious and philosophical movements which claimed inner illumination ; these
he regarded as mere opinionated self-confidence. Such a
faith, he says, is destructive of reason and " substitutes in
its room the ungrounded fancies of a man's own brain, and
assumes them for a foundation both of opinion and conduct ".
The empiricism with which Locke confronted such beliefs
is perhaps the only antidote of permanent value to the out-
breaks of mysticism, irrationalism, confused verbalising, and
pretentious profundity by which philosophers are infected
from time to time. It is his contention that we must at all
costs separate reasonable convictions from " inclinations,
fancies and strong assurances ". Illumination without search
and certainty without proof, are not the evidence of faith
but of a weak credulity. " And he that takes away reason
to make way for revelation puts out the light of both, and
does much the same as if he would persuade a man to put
out his eyes the better to receive the remote light of an
invisible star by a telescope."

What Locke is really saying is that it is the right and duty
of the individual to criticise, question and discover for himself
in terms of direct experience via the senses or logical reflection
thereon.

There is an interesting corollary to Locke's theory. What
happens if we seek to go beyond the necessary limits of the
understanding, if we try to use reason to perform tasks
beyond its power and to answer questions to which experience
can offer no solution ? The result will be confusion. But
if we conclude from this that reason is a useless method of
finding the truth, we are in error. Reason can find out all
the truth that is available and all, therefore, that we really
need to know. This should be enough for us. Further
truth is unobtainable. If knowledge based upon experience

cannot answer all the questions we should like resolved, we should stop asking such questions and not criticise reason.

THE MIND BEFORE EXPERIENCE

Locke believed that before impressions from the outside world fell upon it, the mind was a blank sheet, a *tabula rasa*. We gain knowledge by accumulating sensations and building up ideas on the basis of this experience.

In this Locke was wrong. We always come to experience with some critical interest, asking some question, looking for something, and with a mind which apprehends facts through certain ways of seeing and understanding, just as a botanist looks at flowers from his own trained point of view, which is different from the way an artist or a poet would look at them. To this criticism we shall return when we are discussing Kant.

PRIMARY AND SECONDARY QUALITIES

Locke held that we perceive in any object two kinds of qualities. The colour and sound which we perceive are effects *in the mind* of the physical stimuli derived from material things. The retina is excited by light waves which are themselves colourless movements, the retina then produces disturbances in the brain which give us the sensation of colour. This is a *secondary quality*.

The object itself has solidity and shape, which we discover by touch, and these are the *primary qualities*. It is the material object, thus known, which produces the physical stimuli which reach the retina and ultimately the brain.

Only the sensations of solidity, shape, size, etc., truly represent the qualities of the material object; the sensations of colour do not. There is no colour in the object, but only a certain kind of motion of the material substance which produces the sensation of colour in the mind.

The consequences of this view were not realised by Locke

and hardly seem consistent with common sense.   As Whitehead wittily says :

> The bodies are perceived as with qualities which in reality
> do not belong to them, qualities which are in fact purely
> the offspring of the mind.   Thus nature gets the credit
> for what should in truth be reserved for ourselves : the
> rose for its scent, the nightingale for his song, and the
> sun for his radiance.   The poets are entirely mistaken.
> They should address their lyrics to themselves and turn
> them into odes of self-congratulation on the excellency of
> the human mind.   Nature is a dull affair, soundless, scent-
> less, colourless, merely the hurrying of material, endlessly,
> meaninglessly.[1]

DO QUALITIES INHERE IN SOME SUBSTANCE ?

Locke held that the qualities revealed by touch assure us
of the existence of a material object.   But what were they
the properties of ?   His answer was that there must be a
quality-less ground base, or *something*, in which these primary
qualities inhere and appear together.   This has been called
' the pin cushion ' theory, because the qualities we sense are
supposed to be stuck in the impalpable substance, *and to
depend on it*.   But clearly we can never get at it, since we only
sense the qualities produced by it.   Berkeley's view was that
we should dispense with the unknown and inapprehensible
substance and be content with the qualities.   The thing itself,
he said, *is* its qualities, and of these qualities, those of shape
and solidity are as *mental* as those of colour and sound.

THE THEORY OF REPRESENTATIVE PERCEPTION

Locke, then, was not in a position to demonstrate that we
actually perceived material objects.   We are only aware of
the primary qualities of size and hardness, known by sensa-

---

[1] A. N. Whitehead, *Science and the Modern World.*

tions, and we never perceive the substance on which they inhere. Now Descartes had said that " all the objects of knowledge are ideas in my own mind ", and that the mind knows itself more certainly than it knows objects. But is not Locke also saying that the direct objects of knowledge are sensations *in the mind* even though they *represent* truly the *physical* qualities of solid objects ? If this is so, we have no direct knowledge of anything but the contents of our own minds. Locke, of course, did not draw this conclusion, because he was not in the least concerned with the interaction of mind and body, but was simply asserting that knowledge is based on sense experience. A philosophically sound theory of perception would have enabled him to avoid this error, which does not invalidate his general argument. Berkeley, however, was very much concerned with this problem and was to take it up with surprising results.

GEORGE BERKELEY (1685-1753)

Berkeley, the Bishop of Clone, was deeply concerned with the conclusions that were being drawn from Locke's theory. It appeared, according to Locke, that the only valid knowledge was that based on sensations derived from *material objects*. This gave encouragement to materialism, even if Locke himself did not think so. Berkeley was alarmed, but when he read Locke for himself he discovered in Locke's distinction between primary and secondary qualities, and in his theory of representative perception, not only grave philosophical errors, but positions which, if developed, refuted materialism and established *idealism*—the view that all reality is at bottom mental. This was a brilliant discovery and it was set forth concisely, clearly and in admirable prose in the Bishop's *Treatise Concerning the Principles of Human Knowledge* and three *Dialogues in Opposition to Sceptics and Atheists*.

Berkeley was able to argue that there was no more evidence for the actual existence of the physical cause of sensation

than for the colour and sound. If we only know of the
existence of matter from sensations, it is impossible to know
whether they represent material objects.

We should, however, be misrepresenting Berkeley if we
implied that he wished us to doubt our experiences of solid,
coloured, real objects. We have these experiences of course ;
all he wishes to do is to take away their material cause.
What, then, is the source of sensation if not material objects ?

To me [says Berkeley] it is evident that sensible things
cannot exist otherwise than in a mind or spirit. Whence
I conclude, not that they have no real existence, but that
seeing they depend not on my thought, and have an
existence distinct from being perceived by me, there must
be some other Mind wherein they exist. As sure, therefore, as the sensible world really exists, so sure is there an
infinite omnipresent Spirit who contains and supports it.

Thus does Berkeley argue for the existence of God.

When Samuel Johnson was confronted with Berkeley's
theory he proceeded to kick a large stone with some violence
and exclaimed, " I refute it thus." He did not refute it ;
nor does anyone refute it who supposes that Berkeley did
not allow him to believe in nature as real and substantial.
Berkeley says :

We are not deprived of any one thing in nature. Whatever we see, feel, hear, or in any wise conceive or understand, remains as secure as ever, and is as real as ever. . . .
That the things I see with mine eyes and touch with my
hands do exist, really exist, I make not the least question.
The only thing whose existence we deny, *is that which
philosophers call matter.*

Why, then, do we perceive these things ?

It is plain, says Berkeley, that they have an existence
exterior to my mind, since they are independent of it in the

sense that I cannot believe what I like, I am *compelled* to believe what my senses tell me. Also it is true that things exist during the intervals between the times of my perceiving them, how can that be ? The explanation is that they exist "*in some other Mind*" and it is this Mind which is the real source of all sensations, affecting the individual at every moment with the sensations he perceives. In other words " the things by me perceived are known by the understanding, and produced by the will of an infinite Spirit ".

We may call this form of idealism *Objective Idealism*. Berkeley does not say that we only know ourselves ; we do indeed know away from ourselves, but what we know are *objective mental objects*, not material objects.

BERKELEY AND THE SCIENTIFIC WORLD

Berkeley is an empiricist. Like Locke, he bases all his knowledge on experience, even if it is only mental experience. How he proves the existence of God is another matter ; actually he cannot do without God to maintain some kind of an independent and external world. He cannot maintain his theory without a God who is the source of our sensations.

We thus have two very different forms of empiricism. The first insists that all beliefs should be based on observation and tested by further observation and experiment. All science is empirical in this sense. But the second form, which also derives from Locke (and Hume) but owes much to Berkeley, contends that science should confine itself to observations of fact, reducing its findings to rules and predictions of the order of human sensations, and should avoid theories which substitute speculations about imperceptible entities for the study of the observed regularities of perceptible events. As this would rule out the atomic and electronic theories of matter and all basic explanatory theories, it is not accepted by science in general.

BERKELEY'S INFLUENCE

Since many who were convinced by his arguments against Locke could not accept his view that God was the source of our sensations (on the grounds that the same arguments by which he tried to show that we have no right to assert the existence of substance, would also show that we had no right to assert the existence of God), the conclusion drawn was that we only perceive our own ideas and that the external world is a sort of dream, wholly within our own minds. This is Solipsism.

Others, however, believed that both the subject and the object of knowledge are equally real and equally manifestations of Absolute Mind. Like Plato, they believed that universals had their being independent of the knowing mind. These are objective idealists.

The most persistent consequence of Berkeley's argument is a subjective idealism which he himself escaped by making God the source of our ideas. This most often manifests itself as a tendency to disbelieve in the material world and to accept the idealist conception of the world as Mind, spirit, thought. This, as Berkeley realised, removed most of the objections to revealed religion. It remains to be seen whether Idealism as a philosophy can be acceptable to orthodox theology.

THE REFUTATION OF IDEALISM

Certain objections have been advanced to Berkeley's position and to the subjective idealism to which it seems to lead. In 1903 G. E. Moore published his essay on *The Refutation of Idealism*, and in 1925 a further study entitled *A Defence of Common Sense*. Moore argued that when philosophers declare that material things do not exist, they are denying not only what every sane man knows to be true, but what these philosophers themselves know to be true, for they know that they themselves have material bodies and so have the other philosophers they are trying to convince that bodies do not exist. It is strange, says Moore, that philosophers have been able to hold sincerely, as part of their philosophical creed, propositions inconsistent with what they themselves know to be true.

Professor Wisdom has advanced a somewhat similar argument. There is something very odd, he says, about the situation when a philosopher says " I don't believe that this material table exists ". If when you are seeking water in the desert someone gazes at what looks like water in the distance and says " I doubt whether there is really water there ", *that* is not absurd. But the philosopher says " I don't believe this is real water " *while he is drinking it*, he says it when no one but a madman or a philosopher would ! If a man really feels like this about material things, then he has a defective sense of reality and is usually removed to a home. But in fact, as Hume was to point out, the moment he takes up the affairs of life he entirely forgets his idealist philosophy and behaves like everybody else.

DOUBTS ABOUT IDEALISM

Idealism really springs not from Berkeley but from Locke and his theory of representative perception. If it is believed that what we perceive are sensations, and, assuming this, we seek to prove that they are derived from material objects, we shall never do so. We have begged the whole question in our assumption. We have no grounds for saying that we perceive sensations. We perceive material *objects*. The fallacy is more easily seen if we realise that because we cannot think of a thing without having an idea of it, that does not mean that we can only think of the idea. Similarly the fact that we can only perceive by means of sensations does not mean that we only perceive sensations ; we perceive the material object. It does mean that how we perceive the object is determined by and limited by the range of our sensations and the conditions under which they operate. All knowledge of the object is thus relative, but it is always about what is outside of and independent of ourselves. And there is no reason, in the recognition of this relativity, to question the existence of a material object. It is a very good reason for believing that our knowledge is always partial, relative and conditioned. But it is still true as far as it goes ; and it certainly goes far enough to assure us of its materiality.

12

Hume and Kant

DAVID HUME (1711–76)

THE Scottish philosopher David Hume, historian, diplomat and man of the world, carried empiricism to its logical conclusion, and in so doing revealed its inadequacy. Locke had believed that primary qualities inhered in a material substance, Berkeley believed that sensations inhered in a spiritual substance, the mind. Hume pointed out that if, as Berkeley said, a thing was no more than the sum of its qualities and needed no material substratum, then a mind was no more than the succession of its sensations and these needed no spiritual substratum, no 'mind' to dwell in. When I look into the mind, he says, I only see actual perceptions, never the mind which perceives them. The ego cannot be directly perceived.

If this is so, knowledge is not a subject object relationship, for there is no subject and no object, but only a succession of sensations. Of course like all idealists Hume knows that the object really exists but, on Locke and Berkeley's view of our sensations, he does not see how it is possible for us to know it !

THE NATURE OF CAUSATION

Hume went on to show that it also followed inevitably from the empiricist theory that knowledge is a succession of sensations in the mind, that it was impossible to believe in *causation.* How do we know that one thing is the cause of another? We never perceive the cause passing over into the effect. We only see one thing followed by another; and if this is constantly repeated, we come to *expect* the second whenever the first occurs. This is psychological expectation, not causal connection.

It follows that if we have only empirical facts, only individual things, only one thing after another, then we can find no general laws but only summaries of events, lists of observed regularities. There can be no knowledge of the structure of the world, no *reliable* relation of one fact to another.

Later John Stuart Mill, who was also an empiricist, attempted to justify the validity of inductive logic, which arrives at general laws from particular instances. He failed to do so. As Whitehead says, on empiricist principles

> we must not ascribe, we must not expect, one step beyond our direct knowledge. The (empiricist) has no foothold on which to rely for speculation beyond the region of direct observation. There is no probability beyond the region of direct observation.[1]

A regular succession is not a sufficient reason for believing in the inevitability of that succession continuing, it only accounts for our *expectation.* We must have a better reason for believing that night will always follow day than the fact that in our experience it has always done so. The real reason, as we know, is the rotation of the world on its axis. But this is a scientific theory and could never be deduced from any number of mere observations. Hume made no attempt to explain how far-reaching scientific theories of this kind can be inferred from such data.

Hume's devastating scepticism led him to reject all knowledge or claims to knowledge other than mathematical truths

[1] Whitehead, *Adventures of Ideas.*

(which are not, of course, derived from experience and are independent of the actual world) and matters of fact.

> When we run over our libraries, persuaded of these principles, what havoc must we make? If we take in our hand any volume; of divinity or school metaphysics, for instance; let us ask, Does it contain any abstract reasoning concerning quantity or number? No. Does it contain any experimental reasoning concerning matter of fact and existence? No. Commit it then to the flames: for it can contain nothing but sophistry and illusion.[1]

COMMON SENSE PREVAILS

We have no reason to believe that Hume believed any of his conclusions in a practical sense. They were the intellectual conclusions which followed from certain premises, then generally accepted. What he was really saying was: How can we know what in fact we are quite sure of if we accept the empiricist theories? Hume had no alternative theory of knowledge to offer us. Fortunately, although on these principles one cannot defend reason by reason, or believe in the existence of the body, Nature has seen to it that we do not have to depend for our belief in these things on philosophical arguments. We have to take these things for granted: " Nature will always maintain her rights, and prevail in the end over any abstract reasoning whatsoever."

Hume is leading us astray here. When you reason in such a way as to reach absurd conclusions, you should not abandon reason for a non-rational way of finding reality; you should criticise the *method of reasoning* you are using, and learn to reason better.

HUME ON RELIGION

Hume's devastating scepticism was turned next to religion.

[1] Hume, *An Inquiry Concerning Human Understanding.*

" Examine the religious principles which have, in fact, prevailed in the world. You will scarcely be persuaded that they are anything but sick men's dreams." He criticises miracles on the ground that it is always more likely either that the event has been misreported, or that it is susceptible of a natural explanation, than that a miracle has occurred.

But once again, like the Nominalists, he argued that we do not have to disbelieve because reason cannot substantiate religious truth. We can believe on other than rational grounds. To base our beliefs on reason is indeed dangerous because it lays one open to refutation and consequent loss of faith. One must therefore believe on the basis of pure faith or in revelation, which no argument can overthrow. " To be a philosophical sceptic, then, is the first and most essential step towards being a sound, believing Christian." [1] This rather cynical remark Hume, presumably, did not intend his readers to take seriously.

HUME AND THE EVERYDAY WORLD

It is important to realise that whatever argument he was pursuing Hume was never truculent, never contemptuous of his opponents' opinions, never bitter. He was calm, logical, urbane and always ready, with a shrug, to laugh off his conclusions and affirm that the moment he rose from his arguments and walked out into the street he found himself " absolutely and necessarily determined to live, and talk, and act like other people in the common affairs of life ", and on returning to his philosophical speculations " they appear so cold, and strained, and ridiculous, that I cannot find in my heart to enter into them any farther ".

HUME AND METAPHYSICS

When all was said and done he had, however, convinced

[1] Hume, *Dialogues Concerning Natural Religion.*

a great many thoughtful people, and among them the German philosopher Kant, that

> The vast majority of human opinions are, and always have been, worthless and devoid of validity. Reasoning, however shrewd and persistent, directed upon the feeble and fallacious products of the imagination, and reasoning wasted ; and all edifices of thought erected upon no firmer basis than this are subjective shiftings, mischievous superstitions, pseudo-sciences, houses built of cards.

KANT (1724–1804)

Kant was born and died in Königsberg in East Prussia. He scarcely travelled 40 miles from the city in his lifetime, living a quiet, retired life of great regularity. He was called to the chair of logic and metaphysics in the University in 1770 ; and from his study there issued a series of important works which entirely transformed European thought.

Leibniz had been followed by a dull and pedantic philosopher named *Wolff*, who taught that ideas on the one hand and science on the other could both be developed into entirely rational systems, and that the two systems were harmonious ; moreover, the truths of both provinces were discoverable *a priori* (independently of experience), and both manifested the Divine purpose. Science was thus united with theology, the world being conceived as a huge mechanism designed to serve divine ends.

His philosophy was thus decidedly fatalistic in its attitude. This did not please Frederick William I of Prussia, who was told that if his grenadiers deserted they could not help themselves, since everything, according to the philosopher, happened by necessity and with sufficient reason. Wolff was dismissed ; but the king, doubtless realising that no one was likely to take this philosophy seriously, recalled him in 1688.

This form of Rationalism was a radical departure from medieval thinking, which, at this time, increasingly appeared to be mere obscurantism, so that the philosophical movement which thus developed was known as the Enlightenment. It had, however, a Romantic as well as a Rationalistic aspect. If Spinoza, Leibniz and Wolff were rationalists, Lessing and a number of literary figures developed certain aspects of the teaching of Leibniz in a quite other direction, seizing on his conception of reality as essentially dynamic, alive to the last monad, and increasingly doubtful about the sufficiency of reason to explain everything in human life.

The Enlightenment in England had also departed from Rationalism, but, still in the name of reason, sought to substitute for authority and the traditional philosophy of the Middle Ages, a new philosophy based on hard facts and experience. Voltaire had popularised Locke all over the Continent, and Hume's sceptical conclusions had penetrated into all the universities of Europe.

Both tendencies made their impact on Kant, who had begun his career as a follower of Wolff. Hume's scepticism woke him from his dogmatic slumber. Kant writes :

> Since the origin of metaphysics so far as we know its history, nothing has ever happened more decisive to its fate than the attack made upon it by David Hume. He challenges reason, and demonstrates that there is not and cannot be any such thing as metaphysics at all.[1]

Hume had also rejected causation and the knowledge of a material world—asserting that all we had experience of was sensation.

Then Rousseau made clear to him the sovereign importance of *feeling*. While Kant himself was determined to find a philosophical justification for the demands of the moral sense and religion. (He was a deeply pious man.)

Kant came to realise that if the scientific reason cannot give us the great truths of religion, neither can the scientific

[1] Kant, *Prolegomena*.

reason give us *reality* in itself, but only reality as modified, filtered, distorted by the way in which we *have* to think. But if reason cannot find reality, there is another faculty that indubitably does. As authoritative as science in its field was the intuitive voice of conscience in the field of morals. We cannot escape it, or deny its authority. To Kant, conscience became the one point of experience in which we touch absolute reality. It is, in fact, the call of reality within the individual mind. Was he then to take the easy road of rejecting reason for intuition ? He could not do this, because, though reason was inadequate in dealing with moral obligations and religion, it was surely the basis of scientific thought, and Kant was determined to safeguard the rights of science, which he valued highly, and to vindicate its authenticity in the face of Hume's scepticism. Kant's solution was masterly. He discovered not only how to vindicate scientific reason in the face of Hume's rejection of causation and of knowledge of the external world, but to do so *by such an argument as would simultaneously vindicate religion.* He did this by showing that the mind is an instrument *so constructed* as to apprehend bare facts always in rational form. We cannot know (rationally) anything unless we know it as an object possessing qualities. We cannot know an orderly sequence of events except as causally connected. But reason (*Verstand*, as Kant called it) of this sort has a limited function. It deals only with phenomena, with sense knowledge. If it is applied to metaphysical problems it breaks down and gives nonsensical and contradictory results. If it is used to prove the existence of God, it totally fails to do so. It is not the instrument for these particular purposes.

Is there any way, then, of approaching reality other than by this limited but necessary and useful mechanism of the scientific reason ? Yes, indeed. There is another kind of reason (*Vernunft*, as Kant called it), which grasps underlying truths, which apprehends things in their connection, in their unity, which transcends the conditions of ordinary experience.

Ordinary knowing can give us objects in time and space, causally connected, but we need a higher kind of knowledge to make phenomena intelligible, connected, purposeful. For this we use what he calls *regulative* ideas. He means that things look AS IF they were intelligible when you interpret them in the light of certain principles (of causality, substance and reciprocity). There could be no systematic unity of experience, no consciousness of a world of objects and events all related as parts of one space and one time, unless these principles regulated and controlled the operations of consciousness. But that doesn't mean that they actually *are* what our regulative ideas make them out to be.

Ordinary knowing gives us objects as seen scientifically and as such they are *phenomena*, that is to say things as they appear to us using the instrument of scientific reason, but that does not mean that they reveal the thing *as it really is, in itself*, apart from being so apprehended. We cannot in point of fact *know* things (in this sense) directly ; we always and necessarily see things from a particular angle, through the distorting mechanism of the mind.

It follows that the world around us, as we experience it, is not just simply *there* as we experience it. It is very largely made by us, because what we experience is not simply what our sense organs react to, but is a selection, handled, manipulated, processed and grouped (even packaged) by the operations of the mind.

THE HIGHER REACH OF THE MIND

But the fact that the scientific reason gives us a mechanical world and not metaphysical truth, causality and not freedom, material phenomena and not morals and religion, does not rule these things out. Scientific reason cannot give us these simply because it is limited to its own job.

What we need to do if we want to find the moral law,

freedom and religion, is to open up the way to another kind of knowledge, that is *not* the way of science. This is by *using* the actual *sense of obligation* and also the *feeling for beauty*, as valid in themselves; as having as much validity in their own way as reason has in its way.

As Kant put it,

From the critical point of view the doctrine of morality and the doctrine of science may each be true in its own sphere, which could never have been shown had not criticism previously established our unavoidable ignorance of the real world, and limited all that we can *know* scientifically to mere phenomena. I have therefore found it necessary to deny *knowledge* of God, freedom and immortality, in order to find a place for *faith*.

There is thus a higher road to truth above the impure knowledge of the senses, independent indeed of sense experience, a faculty belonging to us by the inherent nature of the mind. Kant says that we have learnt to distinguish between the faculty of thinking the true through knowledge, and the faculty of intuiting the good through feeling; and these two must not be confused with one another.

The *a priori* principles of morals are as absolute and certain as those of mathematics, and are not derived from experience. The commands of duty are categorical and indisputable. We do not have to find a rational proof to establish this, we *start* from this as datum, and reason thereafter. We do and must act from a sense of moral obligation, we do and must feel religious reverence, we do and must respond to beauty. Accepting the fact that we need not be put off by the inability of scientific reason to prove their validity or deal with them, which would be unreasonable, as Kant has shown, we may now proceed to reason *about* these indubitable experiences.

CRITICISM

1. The fact that our minds *select* and work with the concepts and categories of reason need not shut them off from reality. It means that what they know is *partial*, but not that we do not know reality itself. We know those aspects of it which our way of thinking is able to handle, and the validity and objectivity of that knowledge may be tested by further observation, experience and experiment.

2. The methods and categories used by the mind vary according to the subject-matter. We are compelled to use special ways of thinking, special methods of selecting, classifying and handling whether we are studying physical science or biology, biology or psychology, psychology or medicine, whether we apply our minds to anthropology or sociology. In all these spheres we use forms of the scientific reason, but different forms, and in all these spheres we find aspects of reality itself.

3. Intuition is not confined to the higher reaches of the mind and reason is not limited to the lower and more material reaches. Scientists cannot do without intuition in framing hypotheses, and philosophers cannot do without reason to test their intuitions. *Both* are essential at every level, and without them there is no explanatory knowledge at all. When Kant separates critical knowledge from intuition he opens the door to a torrent of illusions and fables and superstitions. But he has no need to limit reason in order to make room for faith. Faith is needed by the scientist, but must be tested by reason. Only that faith which stands the test of reason, i.e. verification by subsequent experience, and integration with the total corpus of ascertained knowledge, is valid.

13

Hegel 1770–1831

FIFTY years before Darwin's *Origin of Species* was published in 1859, Georg Wilhelm Friedrich Hegel had reached the view that the world was in process of development. He arrived at this conclusion, however, not, like Darwin, by a painstaking investigation of nature but by pure thought.

He lived in a singularly stirring age. From all sides tremendous experiences were crowding in upon men, challenging their accepted beliefs, enlarging their view of the world, shaking them out of their habitual grooves of feeling, thought and action. The powerful forces unchained by the French Revolution, with its magnificent ideals of liberty, fraternity and equality, and its terrible excesses, had their reflection in the philosophy of these years. It was an age abounding in great men—great generals, great statesmen, great poets, great philosophers ; but, at the same time, these eminent individuals were vividly conscious of a destiny not of their own making or choosing, of being the tools of spiritual forces working through them, of which they could not grasp the full nature nor foresee the ultimate effects. When Hegel saw Napoleon riding through the streets of Jena he declared that he had met " the world-spirit on horseback ". But for Hegel all the literary, scientific and political movements of his time, no less than the men through whom these movements were focused, were manifestations of the world spirit, of the Absolute.

Hegel lectured at Jena and Heidelburg and finally settled in Berlin in 1818. Most of his writings consist of lecture notes or notes taken by his students. Only the *Logic* and the *Phenomenology* are from his own hand. His principal works in addition to these are the *Philosophy of Mind*, the *History of Philosophy*, and the *Philosophy of Right*. He died suddenly of cholera in 1831.

His principal followers in this country were Caird, Green, Wallace, McTaggart, Bosanquet and Bradley. In Italy his work was both criticised and continued by Benedetto Croce. In the United States the most important follower of Hegel was Josiah Royce. The German Hegelians entered the sphere of religion and wrote critical studies on the Bible and the Life of Christ; but their most influential representative was Karl Marx.

Hegel was often extremely obscure and his system is not only complex but often incomprehensible to the ordinary mind. When the English philosopher Hutchinson Stirling tried to expound him in his book *The Secret of Hegel*, one of his critics remarked that the secret had been well kept!

It would be unwise to attempt to throw light on Hegel by summarising already largely unintelligible summaries, but we can, perhaps, by a very free treatment, ruthlessly omitting technical details and large portions of the argument, emphasise the living spirit of Hegel's philosophy and show its bearing on life and history.

THE WORLD SPIRIT AND PHILOSOPHY

The Hegelian system is the story of the appearances or manifestation of the Absolute, of Idea, of Spirit; it is therefore the analysis of every form of spiritual life through which that manifestation takes place. In philosophy this process becomes conscious of itself and of the *identity* of the Spirit which underlies such diverse experiences.

Hegel is sometimes regarded as the most abstract of all philosophers, especially by those who first read his *Logic*. He is in fact the most concrete of philosophers, because the actual world of appearances is precisely the appearance and manifestation of Reality. Hegel is totally unlike Kant for whom appearances masked reality; for Hegel Reality did not lurk, the great unknown, behind phenomena. When we speak of the world *as we perceive it*, on the one hand, and the world *as it discloses itself*, on the other, both phrases mean the same thing for Hegel. Our ideas *are* the facts. That which we perceive and think is not different from, but identical with, the real world. Reality reveals itself, or some aspect of itself, in all our experiences.

For Kant the inadequacy of the world as perceived was that our perceptions distorted what they represented, acting as an opaque screen between ourselves and the theory-in-itself. For Hegel a limited experience is true enough in its limited context. A closer approximation to reality is obtained not by going behind it but by extending its range on every side, in other words, by taking more associated things into account. This is sheer common sense. To understand a man we need to know not what he has just done or said but something of his antecedents, his background, his associates, his position, and so forth.

Now all the experiences of the world together, not merely mine but everybody's, if made as complete and coherent as possible, give us the Universe, Reality, the Absolute.

It follows that the ideal of philosophical knowledge is *comprehensiveness* and *systematisation*.

REALITY IS MEANING

Let us return for a moment to the statement that ideas *are* the facts of the world. If this is so, then *thought* is *reality*.

Is that so ? To get this clear we should understand Hegel as saying that reality is meaning ; it is found therefore not in bare sensations, but in *interpreting* this, by finding the relations and meaning of the limited experience by relating it to a wider whole. As a biologist comes to understand such an animal as a frog by showing that it is a sort of improved fish (actually it *is* a fish as a tadpole), and also that it is a reptile and a mammal in the making.

To put it otherwise, the more rational we make the facts the more real they are. The rational is the real and the real is the rational. Hence we get a growth of reality in the development of thought and science. If we want to understand this *identity* of rational ideas and reality we must say that thought is not that which thinks but *that which it thinks*. Ideas for Hegel don't exist only in people's heads. They get into our heads when we think and are themselves independent of people's thinking. Reality is outside us to start with, but gets into our heads as our ideas about it get clearer.

RELATEDNESS

No particular thing, then, is fully real. It involves a context. The more isolated, the less real. The whole is more real than the parts taken separately. An individual is the expression of the society in which he occurs. His every act is determined by his biological inheritance, his own past experience and his present environment. Only the whole is completely real. The Real is both universal in the comprehensiveness of its range and concrete in actually being the world. So Hegel does not find his universal outside the world, like Plato ; it is *the concrete universal*.

BECOMING

Hegel insists, therefore, that to understand anything we have to consider what it developed *from* and what it is

developing *into*. An egg is to be understood as coming from
a hen, and as a potential chicken. The child is father to
the man; but is himself the offspring of a man; *what* he
is is revealed partly by his origins and partly by the promise
of his subsequent development. Thus Hegel sees not so
much *things* as *processes*; any *thing* is really something in
process of development, something changing. In fact a
thing apart from its becoming is an abstraction.

NATURE AND MIND

Hegel is not an idealist in the sense that he makes Mind
the source of Matter. He is quite clear that mind is a product
of development and change in the natural world. But neither
does he say that the material world is self-sufficient, that it
can get along on its own. On the contrary it is derivative,
it is created by Idea. Idea, however, is *not* Mind. It is
something real in itself and not dependent in any way upon
the mind that thinks it. Nature, then, is in no sense an
illusion, mere appearance, something that exists because we
think it.

But nature is on the move. It is in fact a stage in an
unending process. At any one moment it is incomplete,
unfinished. To consider nature just as it is now, without
realising what it is developing into, is what Hegel calls
abstract thinking. It is abstract because nature *now* has been
separated from what it is becoming, and from what it was,
abstracted from *the sequence of events*, the whole evolutionary
process, in terms of which alone any one stage is seen for
what it *really* is concretely, that is to say. The concrete is
not the particular, but the whole series which gives meaning
to the particular. (This is a point that was subsequently
taken up by Whitehead in his discussion on ' the fallacy of
misplaced concreteness '.)

I regret to say that Hegel proceeded to add mystification
to clarification at this point by arguing that nature not only

produces mind but is *evolving into mind*. What this means exactly no one has been able to say.

We may note in conclusion that though nature is created by Idea it is never separate from it. Unlike Descartes, who separated spirit and matter, Hegel (and Spinoza) united them, they retain a substantial identity.

THE ABSOLUTE

We now come to a piece of pure mythology, but let us not beg the question by assuming that a myth may not embody the truth. Spirit, in order to appreciate itself, must abrogate itself, must lose itself, must wander in a world alien to its nature and come at last to itself again. Nature is this foreign land. Nature is the limitation, the emptying, the otherness of Spirit. The subsequent development of nature is the gradual recovery of what was thus temporarily lost. Thus consciousness at last appears, and consciousness proceeds to realise and externalise all the potentialities of Spirit. Thus Reality gradually appears, the Spirit comprehending itself in its own externalisation and manifestations.

This leaves us with an insoluble problem: *Why is it necessary for the Absolute to alienate itself into the apparently material, in order to get back to what it started from?*

To this no satisfactory answer has ever been given.

CRITICISM OF THE ABSOLUTE

Hegel's insistence on the priority of Idea reminds us of Plato's Realism—the derivation of all particulars from self-subsistent general Ideas, existing prior to and independent of their actual embodiment in space, time and history. Against this view the Nominalists (and Locke) argued that, on the contrary, material facts came first and general ideas were framed by the mind on the basis of experience. Now Hegel seems to have formed the same pernicious habit of turning a temporal existent into an ontological pre-existent ;

that is to say, starting with something concrete he forms a general idea of this class of things and then imagines that it can have an existence of its own prior to the appearance and existence of actual things. Apples and pears are thus incarnations of transcendental FRUIT. This, it has been said, is the trick of producing real rabbits out of metaphysical top-hats; or, again, explaining that when we see things moving, the hidden cause of these movements is to be found in the shadows cast by moving bodies.

THE DIALECTIC

One of the most important Hegelian notions is that which seeks to explain the development of the partial to the complete, the less real to the more real—the emergence of Reality. This is always going on in every department of human life, and in history itself. This process has a sort of logical *form*, or model. Every truth is in itself inadequate and needs to be supplemented by its opposite. A moral principle when given universal application tends to become more harmful than good; a legal principle pushed to extremes creates injustice. This is a sign of the inadequacy of any *single* proposition, the tendency for it is to require the statement of its opposite to complement it. This shows the need of supplementing the inadequacy of partial truths by moving to more comprehensive ones. We do this, however, not by balancing one truth by its opposite, though that is the first step, but by forming a wider generalisation which gathers up both into a new form and thus preserves whatever was good in them. The process does not stop there. The new truth (or synthesis of the opposing statements) in turn requires an opposing truth to complement it, and once again we proceed to a higher synthesis. This process continues until all partial views are taken up into a final, complete truth, the scheme of totality, the Idea or Absolute.

This is rather a formal or logical way of stating the

principle, and clearly if it is to be properly understood, it must be filled out with any number of instances. But Hegel believes that the order and connection of ideas is the order and connection of things, that the actual follows this law. There is a dialectical movement of this kind in our personal lives, in psychology, in religion, in art, in history, in politics. Thought and being follow the same law. Our task is to discover the higher unity that embraces the diversity, the opposition.

CRITICISM OF THE DIALECTIC

It must be said at once that this is altogether too schematic, and just as nature does not emerge from pre-existent Principles or Ideas, so the movement and progress of reality does not follow, is not determined by, the prior movement of logical thought. This is to put the cart before the horse.

As a matter of fact even Hegel himself made little if any use of the scheme outside his *Logic*, and in his remarks on method in thinking its formal aspect is hardly referred to. No thinker of the first rank, however great his debt to Hegel, has ever followed him in adopting this scheme.[1]

But the dialectic is something wider and more realistic than this logical scheme. It points to the contradictions which appear in any subject or at any level of thought and action because experience is inevitably partial and fragmentary. We can seldom say that all the truth is on one side and all the error on the other. Reality cannot be ultimately at war with itself and we need to think again and do some reformulation of the whole problem on a higher level to overcome the contradiction and do justice to both sides.

[1] Certainly not Marx, although one of the common over-simplifications of Marxism reduces it to this scheme of *Thesis*, *anti-Thesis* and *Synthesis*. One would be hard put to it to find any justification for this view in the writings of Marx and Engels themselves.

DIALECTICS AND HISTORY

Dialectics, thought Hegel, is the very law of history. This indeed is one of the most important aspects of Hegelian thought. For Hegel history is the onward march of the Spirit, and the goal of history is *freedom*. This historical process leads mankind from the Asiatic civilisation to the Greek and Roman, out of which, in turn, the Christian world appears, and then this, in its medieval form, is transformed into the Germanic Order. At each stage freedom widens and the individual (always as a social individual) becomes more important. In the highest stage we have the full development of that State which is the actualisation of freedom.[1]

What is important for us is the view that history is the unfolding of the Idea. All history is the history of thought. Historical transitions are logical transitions set out on a time scale. Thus it is the Graeco-Roman *Idea* that gives rise to, organises, informs and determines every detail of the Graeco-Roman civilisation ; and it is because that *Idea* transforms itself by a logical development into the *Idea* of Christendom that the struggles and changes, the wars and great movements of history follow suit.

CRITICISM OF THE DIALECTIC OF HISTORY

Ideas do make history, but where do they come from ? Does Idea in itself initiate the whole process ? Suppose we reverse the whole picture, as the Nominalists and empiricists did when they made the idea dependent on experience, and make the ideas which certainly do control history arise out of the historical situation. In that case how does change take place ? Clearly the situation must change, but can it

---

[1] This is too important a topic to be dealt with in this brief sketch, it is fully and admirably treated by C. L. Wyper in his *Political Thought* (Teach Yourself Books).

change unless ideas change first ?   We are in a dilemma unless we can find something in the development of the social structure (not itself dependent on the appearance of a new world picture, of new ideas) which makes people see the necessity of social reorganisation.   Might not the development of new sources of power, for instance—the steam engine, the dynamo, nuclear power—urgently demand new patterns of society ?   That is a problem which Hegel never solved, and lies outside the province of this book.

THE FUNCTION OF PHILOSOPHY

Philosophy is realisation of the process of unfolding and development, but for Hegel it is *Nachdenken*, literally a *thinking after* things have been done.   Its subject-matter is that which *has* happened, and its sole purpose is the clarification of the happening.   It is wisdom *after* the event.   " Philosophy comes too late to teach the world what it should be . . . The owl of Minerva begins its flight when the evening shadows have already fallen." [1]   What Hegel means, it would seem, is that *all explanation is justification*.   Evil is interpreted as the necessary counterpoint in a metaphysical harmony. It was a disciple of Hegel who later reversed this whole conception when he declared that " Philosophers have hitherto attempted to explain the world ; the real task is to change it." [2]

AFTER HEGEL

The followers of Hegel followed two entirely different roads.   One group stressed the rationality of the Absolute, its perfection and unchangeability.   This made the task of philosophy the reconciliation of man to things as they are ;

[1] The owl of Minerva.   Minerva is the Roman name for Athena, the goddess of all wisdom and knowledge.   The owl was sacred to her, and her emblem and symbol.

[2] Marx, *Theses on Feuerbach.*

among its chief exponents were Bradley, Bosanquet and Josiah Royce.

The other group stressed the dialectic and devoted their attention to the laws of change, to development. This dynamic view was taken up and fused with certain political and economic theories by Karl Marx.

The British school of Absolutists argued that the very conception of rationality implies a rational universe. The principle at work behind all our mental activity demands an extension to include everything. We are working in the light of a principle of which the complete intelligibility of everything and the unification of everything into a perfectly rational system is the full expression. The knowledge of our finitude, our contradictions, our imperfections, implies that we are *already* under the influence of the infinite, the rational, and the perfect. This is what Hegel called ' the leap to rationality '.

If this is true, we shall regard the order we find in nature as the literal presence of a Reason in nature. The world-mind is actually *within* the processes of nature ; and these processes, as science discovers them, are really *mental* processes, forms of reasoning. Thus cause and effect is reason *drawing conclusions* ; the uniformity of nature is steadfastness of purpose in the Eternal Mind. Science, therefore, becomes literally the tracing of the world thought, for the world and all its laws is nothing else than the object of an eternal thought.

THE LEGACY OF HEGEL

Hegel was the last great speculative genius to appear in the history of philosophy. The substance of his dialectic was to enter the very blood and sinew of the century. The spirit of the age was guided by the cult of historical thought which he himself had initiated. No one else has equally mastered the theories of his predecessors, or traced the connection of them in the same manner. Hegel does not fight against these systems, for he regards them as " the presentation of a particular moment or a particular stage in the evolutionary process of the idea ". Therefore not only is every particular philosophy the daughter of its own time, but, being the latest manifestation of the Idea, it is the result of all the systems which have preceded it and must include every permanent truth which they have enshrined. Thus, says Hegel, contemporary philosophy will be the fullest, most comprehensive, and most adequate system of all.

It is to our contemporary philosophies that we must now turn.

14

The British Empiricist Tradition

THE empiricists were all concerned to *do without* any kind of entity or substance or causative agency which was not indispensable; in this they followed William of Ockham. Bacon rejected abstract truth for the discovery of the truths of nature, Locke held that there was nothing in the mind that was not first in the senses, Berkeley got rid of material substance. Whatever his idealism signified as to the *nature* of reality, namely, that it was mental, he was an empiricist both in the sense that he started from experience, the bare fact that our knowledge consists of percepts, and because he *did without* one of the most universally accepted substances, matter. Hume was an empiricist who even did without the mind; and going further eliminated causation—and God (at any rate as knowable by reason).

We may now move on to some thinkers who are much nearer our own time. *Jeremy Bentham* was more a political theorist than a philosopher, but he 'did without' what Locke found indispensable, Natural Law—man's inherent *right* to life, liberty and property. *Hobbes* before him (1588–1679) had based all ethics and social obligation squarely on the *utility* of rules and government. We cannot do without them because if we ourselves are not constrained by law neither are other people. It is safer to put up with the policeman and to obey rules of conduct which keep our neighbours from interfering with us than to do as we like and have other people doing as they like with us. This was Bentham's view too, but he expressed it as the sovereign law of the greatest happiness of the greatest number. This was not, theoretically, the outcome of a spirit of benevolence (though in fact he was a benevolent man), it was the consequence of individual men insisting on the freedom to seek their own welfare, their own pleasure.

Both Hobbes and Bentham, therefore, dispensed with any Natural Law or any supernatural authority either for government or morals. They were frankly utilitarian.

John Stuart Mill actually worked out a system of ethics based on the pleasure principle and called it *Utilitarianism*. In our day the tradition has been well served by Bertrand Russell, whose principle was always " wherever possible, substitute constructions out of known entities for inferences to unknown entities ", with consequences which we shall later investigate. Finally our contemporary philosophers have gone the whole way in ' doing without ' and have almost reached the point of doing without philosophy, reducing it to a discussion as to the meaningfulness or absence of meaning of verbal statements—a summary of their position that will be qualified and amplified later.

JOHN STUART MILL (1806–73)

Mill is one of the most interesting of nineteenth-century philosophers, because in his case we witness the same impact of Romanticism on rationalism that we saw in the case of Kant. Mill was brought up as a strict Utilitarian and a disciple of Bentham. He was indeed designed by his father to assume the prophet's mantle. But at the age of 20 a profound change came over his life. Mill became acquainted with Wordsworth, Goethe, Coleridge and Thomas Carlyle. Coleridge taught him that analysis and reason, taking things to pieces and then putting the bits together again, does not give the truth. The whole must be apprehended intuitively.

Reason only apprehends what it creates; the mind, if it is to know reality, must be imaginatively synthetic. Mill came to feel the truth of this, not only with his mind but with his whole heart, as he read the poems of Wordsworth and the other Romantics.

But Mill was not at all the kind of man to jettison reason for intuition. Like Kant, he was determined to do justice to both. Mill could not believe unless he understood, his emotions had to go with and not against his thinking.

Mill never entirely escaped from empiricism, but he tried. He was an economist and the political economy of the day declared that if in commerce and industry every man sought his own welfare and nothing else, an 'unknown' hand would by a mysterious alchemy bring golden results for humanity out of those leaden acquisitive instincts. This of course was the charter of *laissez faire*. But Mill became convinced that it was *not* working for the good of all men, but only or mainly for the good of some. Learning from Carlyle that the gospel of mammonism and the cash nexus, as Carlyle called these principles, were spreading misery and poverty at one end of the social scale while they created wealth at the other end, he rewrote his *Political Economy* to advocate a juster distribution of wealth, a finer motive than mere money-getting, and the aim of the common welfare.

Next, greatly influenced by his wife (Harriet Taylor), he turned to the topic of *Freedom* and wrote his great classic on that theme, designed to ward off the pressure of mass opinion and government repression from the individual, who was to think freely and act as he chose, with due respect to the equal right of others to the same freedom.

Finally he turned to *religion*. He declared that it was impossible to believe in the existence of God, but he was prepared to discuss the *possibility* of the existence of such a Being who is limited in his power. "The cultivation of an imaginative hope is quite compatible with reserve as to positive belief, and whatever helps to keep before the mind *the ideal of a perfect being* is of unspeakable value to human nature." Poetry is therefore essential to the fullness of our spiritual life—*the poetry of insight is the religion of the unbelieving*. In the last analysis religion is not belief, but the cultivation of the feelings. (Or is it what James was to call a *pragmatic* belief?)

Mill was also dissatisfied with the *logic* of empiricism, especially as it concerned science. How is it possible to arrive at scientific laws on the basis of observation, of the mere cataloguing of facts? Of course, if scientific laws are only summaries of observations, there is no problem. But as science in the nineteenth century developed, it became clear that it was much more. It was interpretative, explanatory, it sought *behind* phenomena for the laws and structure of reality, and these things were not schemata, useful fictions, convenient ways of expressing mere facts, they were *real*. Mill wrote his *Logic* to attempt to show the validity of the transition from fact to explanatory theory. He did not succeed; there is no logical ladder from bare fact to explanatory truth. It was left to modern philosophy of science to succeed where Mill failed. But he knew what the problem was, and that was more than most people knew at the time.

A very engaging characteristic of John Stuart Mill was his intellectual honesty and his great humility. Truth was no single element, he believed, but a gem of many faces, each capable of different, even contradictory appearance. It was impossible to grasp the whole from a single point of view; and, conversely, every honest point of view achieved an aspect of the truth. He fully practised what he believed. He endured criticism and delighted in correction. It was the secret of his personal charm and of his reputation. On one occasion, hearing that Herbert Spencer was going to denounce him in the *Fortnightly Review*, he wrote to him:

" Nothing can be more agreeable to me than to hear that you are going to answer me in the *Fortnightly Review*. I hope you will not spare me."

He always contended, in controversy, that it is the most reasonable rather than the absurdest form of wrong opinion with which one ought to grapple. We stand little chance of discovering what truth such opinions may contain if we merely attack their weaker aspects. This is a sentiment with which all would, on reflection, agree. But Mill not only believed it, effortlessly he practised it. Perhaps that is why he was called " the Saint of rationalism ".

WILLIAM JAMES (1842–1910)

William James, the American psychologist and philosopher, was a remarkable figure. The brother of Henry James the novelist, it was said of them that William wrote psychology like a novelist and Henry wrote novels like a psychologist. James was undoubtedly the creator of modern psychology, and he was also a philosopher who spoke in terms that were not only understood by the plain man but which powerfully excited his interest ; a gift known to few philosophers.

James was an empiricist. As a psychologist he studied experiences, what he so aptly called " the stream of consciousness ". When James came to consider what it was that we actually know, he again replied *experiences*. He did *not* say : material objects. This is mentalism or empirical idealism. It is the affirmation of the identity between thought and being, as Hegel affirmed that identity, but in a different form. For Hegel saw thought and being as a unity, whereas James saw them as an irreducible multiplicity. In other words he was a Pluralist. For him, and others who shared this view, the parts were more important than the whole.

Pluralism is a philosophy of mosaics, of facts in the plural, facts *not* so closely related as to affect one another, determine and even constitute one another. Facts are not welded to other facts in a rational whole ; they are inconsistent with other facts and cannot be harmonised in a rational whole. Facts are arbitrary, jolting, discontinuous, swarming, tangled, muddy, painful and fragmentary. So much for James' Pluralism, which, however, we shall meet again in another form in the philosophy of Bertrand Russell.

Now for his *Pragmatism*—the theory that the true is merely the useful. It was Dewey who elaborated the theory of knowledge implicit in James' empiricism, and at the same time wedded it to James' Pragmatism. Dewey said that the process of knowing was a way of experiencing. We know only in order to alter experience, to control effects in a desirable way. In knowing, a problematic situation is transformed by certain operations which modify that situation. An idea is not a representation of an object, it is a directive to act in a certain way. We are therefore not concerned with objects as antecedent to knowledge, but only with the effective manipulation of experience.

A scientific law is not an uncovering of reality, but a successful procedural technique. That being so, we alter the conception of truth from a reflection of independent, objective reality, to a statement of the factors involved in a successful problem-solving procedure. Truth now is *only* what works. We mean by it nothing else.

James was less interested in this analysis of scientific knowing than in religion. He argued that we cannot know the truth about God, or Freedom, or Immortality. Nor can we disprove these things of course. Yet it is important whether they are true or not. If they are true, then life is enhanced ; if they are not true, we live in doubt and may die in despair. Why not see whether we can live AS IF they were true ? Why not bet on the most optimistic hypothesis ? We can lose nothing. If in the end we are wrong, we have lived our lives hopefully at any rate. If we are right, then we have happiness both in this world and the next. Let us not say we will only believe what can be proved to be true. Let us say that we will see what works, and *call that truth*.

But this is not what we usually mean by ' truth '. Is not ' truth ' correspondence with fact ? James admitted that his kind of truth was not what has generally been called ' truth ', but in his view it was all we have. The true, then, is whatever proves itself to be good in the way of belief ; it is all that by courage and faith we can *make* true.

This has been severely criticised on the following grounds :

1. It is not a definition of truth ; it gets rid of the whole idea of truth.

2. By ' satisfactory consequences ' it means not testing by experiment, comparing the results with some outside criterion, but satisfactory to the *feelings*. But what can be more satisfactory for a man than to go on believing he is wise when he is a fool. The world is full of superstitious beliefs which give people a great deal of satisfaction.

3. To show that a belief works, in this sense, does not do more than explain why it is believed. It really answers the question, why are *false* beliefs believed.

Santayana said of James that " He did not really believe ; he merely believed that one had the right to believe that he might be right if he believed." This may seem a severe criticism to pass on a very vital and stimulating philosopher and a great psychologist ; but Pragmatism has not survived its criticism among philosophers, even if it has among those who practise wishful thinking. Perhaps it points in the direction of a more practical criterion of belief, but it is badly in need of re-formulation. What it requires is, firstly, a better theory of knowledge, accepting the fact that we can know the material world and avoiding the view that we only know sensations ; and secondly, a better account of hypothesis and verification as the approach to the deeper reality behind phenomena, to the world of objective scientific theory regarded as the structure of nature itself.

JAMES AND THE BLOCK UNIVERSE

James was a bitter opponent of the Hegelian Absolute, which he considered the product of purely abstract reasoning which paid scant regard to fact, imposing on the multifarious world of experience an artificial unity. He described it as :

" The absolute block whose parts have no loose play, the pure plethora of necessary being with the oxygen of possibility all suffocated out of its lungs—there can be neither good nor bad, but one deal level of mere fate."

The world, said James, is not a universe, is not One, but simply a great fact wherein manyness and oneness are set alongside. The world cannot be formulated in a single proposition. It is, in fact, a more many-sided affair than the Hegelian idealist allows for. One Mind, even the mind of the Absolute, cannot have a complete view of reality. The facts of life need many ultimate and irreducible points of view to comprehend it.

James denounces the wishful thinking of the monist who seeks for unity at all costs, and affirms an essential multiplicity in which the parts are more important than the whole, and each stands out as a simple fact which is not required by the other facts (as Hegel thought it was), which, indeed, would form a much better system without them. There is something crude, something jostling and fragmentary about the world ; but it is at any rate a world where nothing is determined and anything is possible.

The world of the Hegelian is, on the contrary, a world devoid of possibility, deprived, as James expresses it, of the oxygen of possibility. The results of such a doctrine of unity is a repose similar to that of the mystic absorbed in the divine vision, of quietism of indifferentism in all its forms.

BERTRAND RUSSELL (1872–1970)

Bertrand Russell was an Empiricist and also a Pluralist, and much else besides, but never a Pragmatist. He was a Fellow of Trinity College, Cambridge, and had a long, adventurous and distinguished intellectual career. His books include academic works of great difficulty, if not obscurity, and brilliant popular expositions of sane living, marriage, education and ethics. He learnt much from Leibniz and was like him an atomist, but he rejected the pre-established harmony.

> The most fundamental of my intellectual beliefs [he says] is that the idea that the world is a unity is rubbish. I think the universe is all spots and jumps, without unity and without continuity, without coherence or orderliness, or any of the other properties that governesses love.

Russell was undoubtedly a Pluralist.

Throughout his philosophy he applies the principle of " where possible substituting construction out of known entities for inferences to unknown entities " when it comes to our knowledge of the external world.

Russell does not distinguish physical objects from sensations. Things are collections of sense-data or appearances, patches of brown, feelings of solidity, smoothness, and so forth. If you add together all possible appearances of an object, their sum *is* that object. For example, a star is just the appearances of the star to all possible observers, or the aspects of the star which different people at different places see and which would be thrown on to the sensitised plates of cameras wherever cameras might be. The notion of a " real " star as the source from which these various aspects come and by which they are caused is quite unnecessary and should be given up. Each physical object has such appearances everywhere ; and since sensations are just these appearances or aspects, there is no difference between the physical and the psychical.

This does not explain how we come to believe in common physical objects, the knowledge of which we all share; but Russell points out that if twenty people look at a table there are twenty sets of sense-data, all of them slightly different because of the different angles of vision and for other reasons. The table itself, then, as a common object is each and all of these sets of sense-data and all possible such sets besides.

Similar views have been held by contemporary philosophers known as Realists,[1] who have engaged in endless disputes as to whether when we look at the ceiling we are directly acquainted with " whiteness " itself or only a white expanse of plaster; whether we perceive the physical object or the sense datum (i.e. whatever is given in sensation), whether the sensation of white is literally part of the surface of a physical object and of how it is related to the unsensed parts; or whether it is *not* as a sensation part of a physical object at all, in which case how do we reach the physical object by means of it? Finally, whether an object is really after all a collection of sensations, of feels, whiffs, glimpses from all points of view as Russell holds.

PHENOMENALISM

This is a view we have met before, in Descartes, who said he was more sure of his own mind than anything else and that he only knew his mental states; in Locke, who thought that our sensations *represented* the material world, but that we did not sense that world itself; in Berkeley and Hume, who reduced all known reality to ideas and experiences; and now in Bertrand Russell, who believed that we know sense-data and that there is nothing else but those events which

---

[1] They are *not* Realists in the philosophical sense of believing in principles, general ideas and ideals as having a real existence independent of the human mind.

occur whenever we experience sensations. From the point of view of my experience, these events make up the stream of consciousness ; but since objects are only all possible points of view which go to make up the object, the same events grouped in this way *are* the objects. How are we to call these events ? Are they mental or physical ? They are, says Russell, " neutral particulars ". From one point of view they make up personalities, from other objects.

Having thus got down to rock-bottom, Russell proceeds to consider what can be deduced about the *structure* of his universe of " neutral particulars ". To this problem he brings a new and rigorous system of logic which, he holds, it is one of the principal tasks of philosophy to formulate and operate. This severe intellectual instrument weeds out meaningless ways of thinking about fundamental problems, and illegitimate processes of thought, as drastically as it deals with superfluous entities. Russell calls this *logical analysis,* and as a method of philosophical thought it is being developed by a modern school of philosophers, the " logical positivists ", and he was perhaps the first of our modern philosophers to advocate the ' logical analysis ' which renders so many metaphysical statements meaningless or superfluous. But his sceptical method produces, as he says, " a lessening of fanaticism with an increasing capacity of sympathy and mutual understanding. In abandoning a part of its dogmatic pretensions philosophy does not cease to suggest and inspire a way of life ".

15

Bergson and Whitehead

BERGSON was born in Paris in 1859. A physicist and mathematician by training, his analytical mind led him irresistibly to philosophy. In 1898 he became professor at the École Normale and in 1900 at the Collège de France. In 1907 he won international fame with his *Creative Evolution*.

Bergson is the most poetical of all philosophic writers, making frequent use of metaphor and analogy. Indeed, this becomes a fault, since a simile in his eloquent pages often becomes the substitute for an argument. Bergson uses his great literary skill to present a philosophy which attempts to unfree old habits of thinking and replace them by less stiff and restricting ones.

The rigid forms of thought against which he directs his criticisms are those of an earlier evolutionary philosophy, that of Herbert Spencer, who conceived evolution as little more than an adjustment of the organism to its environment, not as a creative advance. Spencer's theories have since become obsolete largely because the biological approach has replaced the physical, so that the world is seen not in terms of interacting forces but as in process of change.

But Bergson sees the dead hand of mechanism not only in theories of matter and life but also in the very activity of reasoning itself. He therefore finds it necessary, as Kant did, to limit it to where it really belongs, and makes considerable claims for intuition as the faculty wherewith to apprehend ever-changing reality.

Everything in Bergson therefore is to be understood as *reaction* from the misstatements of a mechanistic and rationalistic philosophy. It is because evolution is described *mechanically* that Bergson introduces a Life Force to make it go. It is because reason is conceived as deductive logic, as working with fixed concepts, that it is held to be incapable of dealing with movement and change. Let us anticipate by saying that in each case truth is not found by going to the opposite extreme of one form of error to another, but by understanding evolution as the biologist actually describes it and by understanding reason in all its fullness as more than dead logic, as intuitive understanding as well as deductive logic.

CREATIVE EVOLUTION

Bergson thinks that evolution as mere mechanical unfolding can never give real novelty, but can only reveal what is already there. But the important thing about evolution is that novelty *does* appear. Darwin discusses the origin of new species, and by evolution we now mean not only new species but new orders and genera, new phyla, the evolution of the mammal from the fish (through amphibia and reptiles), of man from the apes, of the living from the non-living. Behind this evolution, says Bergson, there must be a drive, a " vital force ", making ever new experiments.

The principle of emergence, however, makes this vital force superfluous. A new pattern or organisation of existing elements gives us a new entity with unpredictable qualities of its own. One could not predict from the known properties of the two gases oxygen and hydrogen that in their combinations they could give something so utterly unlike them as water. New combinations of the elements of heredity, genes, which are always taking place, can give rise to novel characteristics in plants and animals, and these, in so far as they give the organism wider opportunities and greater freedom, stand the chance of establishing themselves if used to the maximum advantage.

Clearly this is a question for the biologist, the psychologist and the anthropologist. But, as so often, scientific advance impinges on philosophy and demands that inadequate concepts be abandoned and new ones adopted. It is the better part of reason not to use fixed and antiquated concepts when they are outworn, but to forge better ones. If one does not do so and in consequence fails to understand what is happening, there will be a tendency to blame reason as inadequate and resort to some other method of knowing such as intuition.

To illustrate, one cannot comprehend life with the categories of chemistry. What should one do? Clearly it is necessary to use other categories, those of biology which, while they include those of chemistry, pass beyond them. These will prove adequate for the task without resort to non-rational terms.

When we come to mental phenomena these in turn will not be amenable to purely physiological treatment. Once again there is no reason here to abandon scientific reasoning. It is enough to widen its scope by developing the categories of psychology. These pass beyond those of physiology but are none the less rational and scientific.

The antitheses of reason and intuition is typical of Bergson's fundamental dualism, which appears again in the contrast of life and matter, and of vital force and mechanism. In each case we shall find that Bergson is compelled to accept mystical explanations because he himself limits his understanding of the nature of matter on the one hand, and of reason on the other. There is, however, no need to explain life as due to a vital force acting on inert matter if we see that it is matter itself, in a more complex form, which can manifest the properties of life. This is a dualism that thrives on maintaining an erroneous view of the potentialities of matter.

The resort to vitalism is obscurantist and has been

abandoned by all biologists, not because they have reverted to mechanism, to a 'nothing but' philosophy that reduces life to nothing but chemistry and physics, but because they have learned to use concepts and rational (scientific) methods adequate to their subject-matter.

To resort to a vital force is to go back to the Middle Ages when opium was said to cause sleep by its 'soporific property'. It is to substitute a phrase for one's ignorance and then imagine that one has found an explanation.

Moreover, it obstructs science by closing the door to further investigation. Again and again a puzzle in physiology, which vitalists would attempt to solve by invoking a vital force, has subsequently been solved scientifically by further research. Biology is one long story of such successes. Obstacle after obstacle has been overcome, and none of them would have been tackled if vitalism had been accepted. Vitalism has been driven back step by step and it is always the faith of science that the next unsolved puzzle, where vitalism has once again entrenched itself, is as susceptible of solutions as the others.

BERGSON AND REASON

In criticising Bergson's evolutionary theory we have already moved into the second topic, that of reason. Is reason inadequate for its task? Yes, if it is used in a mechanical way. But has it got to be used in this way? Bergson seems to *want* us to think mechanically in order that he may persuade us to abandon reason for intuition. This is a method that thrives upon the errors of bad thinking, that *prefers* bad thinking to good, that rejoices in mistaken reasoning as revealing the inadequacy of reason itself.

But reason in science has this priceless character, that it always provides its own methods of verification, and it does this at every level. Verification by experiment and observation at the physical level has to be replaced by quite other forms, but equally exacting, in biology and psychology. Intuition, relying as it does wholly on its own inner feeling of having apprehended reality, has no method of testing its findings, so that different people often have contradictory intuitions. Of the two roads to truth only that which can be tested is of any use.

Reason may find that, at some stage, it is failing to organise its subject-matter satisfactorily. More and more facts remain unexplained. Does this mean that reason has failed? Not at all. Explanation is never complete; it is endless approximation, and theory should always be open to revision and improvement. Partial knowledge is all that we have; but it is better than no knowledge at all.

Bergson constantly assumes that reason is pure logic and is incapable of making use of intuition. If it were so, it would indeed be incapable of reaching truth. However, reason does make use of intuition, but it never trusts intuition by itself. Every hypothesis is the result of intuition, but every hypothesis must be tested and verified before it is accepted as true. When the two are thus combined, reason can transcend logic and intuition has found a rational criterion.

BERGSON AND FREEDOM

Bergson is right when he says that both a mechanistic universe, one in which every movement is as determined as the movement of billiard balls once set in motion, and a universe moving irresistibly to a predetermined goal, are inconsistent with freedom. Obviously there is no fundamental difference between these conceptions. They are both determinist.

Bergson's alternative is the theory of *absolute creativeness*, in total freedom, freedom that is unconditioned and unmotived.

But this is a completely meaningless idea. If it could occur it would be the irrational act of a lunatic; but nothing is more determined (by obsessions and delusions) than the thoughts and actions of the insane.

Bergson is right to emphasise the creative function of man. Man is a choosing, deciding animal and choice is burdensome, which is why men look worried. Choice is not the certainty of instinct on the one hand or of external constraint on the other. The true conception of freedom is, to use appropriate Hegelian terms, dialectical. One is not free absolutely, but one is free in the only real sense, and in a vitally important sense, when one *understands* what is best to be done. Then one's choice is determined by one's evaluation of the complex situation; and there is no choice that is not so conditioned. But in these cases we are not surrendering to prejudice, obsessions, ignorance, instinct, or the external pressure of forces which are not allowing us to *evaluate* the situation. This alone would be real loss of freedom, implying our failure to understand the conditions and choose accordingly.

It is freedom of this sort that is creative and carries man forward to greater control of nature and new forms of social life.

A CRITICAL ESTIMATION OF BERGSON

In so far as Bergson has shown us the inadequacies of a static reason and a mechanical conception of nature, he has served us well. In so far as he has convinced us that evolution is creative and produces real novelty, he has helped us too. In so far as he has shown us the important place of intuition in reaching new truth, he has revealed an indispensable element of true reasoning. But he has tended to reinforce the tendency, very prevalent in times of confusion and peril, to confound the easy job of feeling deeply about things with the far more difficult job of thinking seriously about them.

In a period like ours when few men can find the familiar

landmarks by which they once moved securely on their way, fear tends to beget emotional instability. At such times the false is easily accepted precisely because these processes of intellectual liberation by which people are restored to sanity have been suspended by the influence of irrationalist philosophers such as Bergson.

WHITEHEAD (1861–1948)

It was James and Bergson who fought to recover the sense of genuine development and change in the world, and who conceived of men as not fulfilling a preordained plan, but actually creating the world by their own initiative as they went forward; so that what the world is going to be is not already given in the Absolute, but, in the words of William James, " will not be known until the last man's vote is counted ".

It has been Whitehead, however, who has formulated at one and the same time a philosophy which embodies the conception of a creative evolutionary process and a criticism of all forms of abstract mechanistic philosophy. He does this not by accepting Bergson's mystical life force, or by accepting the Hegelian mythology of an evolution proceeding within the unchanging Absolute. He achieves his aim by adopting a thoroughly biological or organic conception of the world, which regards it as a becoming, an eternal process, all the past gathered up by it and borne along with it.

Everything is in motion, and in creative advance. In consequence, in the history of civilisation, we see *successive forms of order*, a sequence of social patterns or civilisations, such as those so brilliantly described by Toynbee. It is the function of philosophy to explain the rise of these types of order, the transition from type to type. This is no easy task and Whitehead's metaphysical system is a difficult one to understand, which accounts for his warning that although his writing is enlivened by a subtle and ironic sense of humour he would have us always remember that we must not expect simple answers to far-reaching questions.

Many people cannot make up their minds whether White-head is an obscure philosopher with frequent amazingly lucid intervals, or, on the other hand, a philosopher almost as clear as the profundity of his problems permits.

THE SPLIT UNIVERSE

Whitehead begins by rejecting out of hand all philosophies which divide the world into *appearances* localised in mind or consciousness and a *reality* with its own separate and inaccessible existence.

> Philosophy has been saddled with the problem of deriving the historic world of change from a changeless world of ultimate reality. The final wisdom has been pictured as the changeless contemplation of changeless contemplation of changeless reality. Action is conceived as inferior and concerned with the less real world.[1]

There is no such dualism in nature. Duality *in unity* is implied in all experience, but not dualism. Throughout the universe there reigns the union of opposites which is the ground of dualism, and one of the clearest examples of this is the unity of mind and matter in man. If this is not understood we see bodily substance carried bodily away from the realm of mind and values, where it becomes a mere mechanism, while the world of minds comes to stand for private worlds of perceptions, morals and art.

This dualism is the result of abstracting certain aspects of reality from the rest and treating them as real in themselves, or even as the basic reality, so that the other aspects are regarded as mere appearance or epiphenomena.[2] There are

[1] Whitehead, *Modes of Thought*.
[2] *Epiphenomena.* By-product of a basic process exerting no appreciable influence, as when mind is conceived as a mere glow on the surface of matter.

three ways of doing this : we may abstract from the living whole the physical side and consider it as the only reality, in which case we become materialists ; we may abstract the mental side and discard the physical as a form of mind, in which case we become idealists ; or we may try to explain things in terms of the interaction of two distinct abstractions, matter and mind, which results in dualism. We can only escape from this muddle if we consider mind as a *function* or activity of certain forms of matter, in which case they are as inseparable as the form impressed on wax by a seal, and mind is to the brain what sight is to the eye, its *function*, not a separate stuff.

THE MATERIAL WORLD

Whitehead criticises our conception of the material world as consisting of separate and distinct particles, destitute of colour and similar qualities but possessing fixed properties and in themselves, unless acted upon, not moving.

This is only true as an *abstraction*, it is not what we find concretely. Yet we think we are actually describing the ultimate, concrete fact when we so describe the material world.

Whitehead calls this *the fallacy of misplaced concreteness*, because concreteness is not here at all. The actual, concrete world is a richer, fuller, more interrelated, living and moving thing.

1. All separate forms interpenetrate and affect one another. Everything exists in some organic pattern within which it is what it is and without which it would not be anything.
2. Everything is a patterned movement, a process and not a static item. All substance moves (matter and motion are not two but one), and the way of its movement (in relation to other items) makes the whole what

it is. Apart from pattern mere existence, and mere quantity, giving size or shape or vibration rate, determines nothing.

3. The environment enters into the nature of each thing. Everything exists or moves in a web and there is mutual connection between them, and particularly between the whole and its parts. For instance, the behaviour of atoms in a living body is different from their behaviour outside. Within it their activity makes the *living* processes of the body.

WHAT DO WE KNOW AND WHAT IS IT THAT KNOWS?

The view of mind that was required by the mechanical notion of matter was of course that the world of sensations was totally different from the material world which caused it or of which it was a representation. It was only in this world that nature was known as coloured, as sounding, and so forth, these appearances being localised in mind or consciousness.

Whitehead rejects this view and holds that there is only *one* nature, not a colourless causal material and a coloured representation produced in the mind. The fact that sensation is *relative* to our sense organs and to conditions, of light for instance, does not make it unreal or merely mental. The colour is really *in the object*, but it is *there*, as seen from *here*, under certain conditions. Thus what the object appears to be is not a private experience of our minds, but reveals the qualities of that object as part of the external world as they occur under definite natural conditions. In other words, we must not separate sensations and the sensed and then ask how we get from one to the other. That is precisely the vicious abstraction which must be avoided. The body regulates our knowledge of the world, enabling us to see *so much of it* and no more. We perceive aspects of the world as determined by the range of our senses, just as a wireless set is tuned to pick up certain stations out of all that are on the air. The fact of selection implies neither pure subjectivity, as though we only perceived our sensations, or even such misrepresentation or distortion that we cannot trust our senses. Our senses are perfectly trustworthy as far as they go. Knowledge, then, is a partial vision of a complex of things generally independent of the act of cognition and, when perceived, always perceived relative to special conditions.

THE AGE OF ABSTRACTION

Whitehead points out that by abstracting the purely physical in this mechanistic way great advances were made in science and technology. It was the success of the method that made men feel that this was ultimate reality.

But it did not account for the living organism or for the appearance of mind, or for the values and significance of the world as seen by artist and poet. The Romantic Reaction, as it expressed itself in such poets as Wordsworth, showed us what we must not leave out. Philosophy, too, exists to promote more complete schemes of thought. It is a critique of abstractions.

EVOLUTION

According to the mechanistic assumption, evolution, in a really creative sense, is impossible because the fundamental stuff has fixed properties. The organic view shows that complex organisms with new properties are formed from simpler organisms and that the properties of things change in different conditions, and when organised in new wholes, in new patterns. Evolution has therefore completely outmoded the mechanistic conceptions of the earlier centuries.

Even when organic evolution was accepted it was too narrowly conceived. In the nineteenth century it was mainly concerned with the adaptation of the organism to a fixed environment. Since this means among other things the environment considered as a food supply, the outcome was emphasis on the struggle for existence.

But creative evolution shows us the power of the organism to recreate its own environment. Those organisms are most successful which modify their environment by cooperative enterprise and in such a way as to enhance the life of the community.

CHANGING FORMS OF ORDER

Creativity is the essence of every form of existence. It means selection from all the available possibilities (i.e. potentialities) and the making concrete of the selected possibility. Life is selective appropriation.

Creativity is seen at every level of evolution and is continued in the history of civilisation. It implies a radical change in the world order, in the social system at each step. It is the business of philosophy to explain the rise of these types of order and the transition from one political form to another. In periods of transition the old order is marked by frustration and confusion. This is not to be deplored, it indicates the dawn of a new age. Philosophy should help us to understand the necessity for criticising the static forms of order which belong to the *status quo*, to show how passing and temporary they are, for to construe the new epoch in terms of the forms of order of its predecessor is to see mere confusion.

That is why, although we can endure slow change ; " when for human experience a drastic period of rapid transition comes upon us, human nature passes into hysteria. When fundamental change arrives, for some of us heaven dawns, for others hell yawns open." [1]

CRITICISM

Whitehead's metaphysical system passes beyond the

[1] Whitehead, *Modes of Thought.*

attempted clarities of the above exposition to enlarge upon three concepts which have not found general acceptance.

1. That all material things have a mental as they have a creative aspect.
2. That there are Platonic eternal objects which lure things in their direction and into which they, in a manner, enter when selected by the creative appropriation.
3. That the creative selection of possibilities in a particular direction is due to a subjective aim which emanates from God ; who is the principle of concretion (i.e. that which controls and guides the process of making potentiality actual). God is the eternal urge of desire ; like Aristotle's unmoved mover, he initiates and directs the entire cosmic process through its love for Him.

THE SIGNIFICANCE OF THE CREATIVE URGE

The philosophy of Whitehead as he advocates it for our day and age is well summed up in his *Adventures of Ideas.*

Systems, scientific and philosophic, come and go. Each method of limited understanding is at length exhausted. In its prime each system is a triumphant success : in its decay it is an obstructive nuisance. The transitions to new fruitfulness of understanding are achieved by recurrence to the utmost depths of intuition for the refreshment of imagination. In the end—though there is no end—what is being achieved, is width of view, issuing in greater opportunities. But opportunity leads upwards or downwards. In unthinking Nature " natural selection " is a synonym for " waste ". Philosophy should now perform its final service. It should seek the insight, dim though it be, to escape the wide wreckage of a race of beings sensitive to values beyond those of mere animal enjoyment.

16

Philosophy Today

WHITEHEAD has escaped from the stage of thinking that the great philosophers were all wrong into the stage of seeing that they were again and again right, though not always in the way their followers thought they were. Our modern world looks back on 2,500 years of philosophical inquiry. What do we make of it?

In his *History of Western Philosophy* Bertrand Russell says that "ever since men became capable of free speculation, their actions, in innumerable important respects, have depended upon their theories as to the world and human life". But unfortunately almost all the questions of most interest to speculative minds "are such that cannot satisfactorily be answered", and contemporary philosophers, abandoning the age-old philosophic quest, confess frankly that "the human intellect is unable to find conclusive answers to many questions of profound importance to mankind". This lack of conviction, of clarity respecting the significance of life, clearly indicates that something is happening to the Western Spirit.

PHILOSOPHICAL ANALYSIS

One reason for this is undoubtedly the appearance of a new school of philosophy in Britain and America, which has been called the school of Philosophical Analysis. Although new, it has its roots deep in the British empiricist tradition, especially in the philosophy of Hume, and it has declared that metaphysical systems have no validity and that questions as to the purpose of human life are meaningless.

Philosophical Analysis holds that all knowledge must be based on experience, and speculative system-building is illegitimate. Many members of this school would also hold that knowledge based on experience can serve only to correlate observations and can tell us nothing of the structure of reality beyond sense-data. This is the philosophical position known as *phenomenalism*, and from it there flows not only a rejection of any claim to know the real world but of any attempt to frame a world view, a philosophy of life; for it follows that the world is nothing but a personal construction of sense data. This is to deny our knowledge of the actual structure of the world and its explanatory laws, of the objective system of nature. Such scepticism throws doubt on our power to change the world, and on the validity of any theory which seeks to understand world development and history. Hence the denial of the possibility of metaphysics, of any total world view.

WORLD VIEWS AND METAPHYSICS

Ignoring the plain fact that phenomenalism is itself a very definite metaphysic, let us turn to the wider question of the capacity of the human mind to answer such fundamental questions as whether the world is basically material, or mental, or both (dualism); as to the relations of body and mind, of freedom and necessity; or as to what kind of purpose, if any, we can find in existence. Not all analysts are phenomenalists, but they would all answer pretty much in the following way: If we are only aware of empirical facts, then apart from logic and mathematics, which concern the manipulation of symbols and tautologies,[1] knowledge cannot pass beyond such facts and no statement of any kind is allowable

[1] *Tautologies*, repetition of the same meaning in different words.

which cannot be verified by an appeal to experience (or is *in principle* capable of being so verified). Now most philosophical statements and attempts to explain or characterise the world are incapable of such verification, therefore they are inadmissible.

The same conclusion may be arrived at in a different way. If we carefully examine the *language* used by philosophers we shall find that it is largely the ambiguities of language, the misuse of language, that are responsible for the difficulties of philosophical questions. If we straighten out the language the question disappears. In fact, a large number of philosophical statements and puzzles are, when analysed, *meaningless*. Language, which is the instrument of thought, is itself deranged: the machinery is out of order. The wheels revolve, the parts grind one against the other, they have all the appearance of working at full pressure; but nothing is produced. If I ask the question: *Is it five o'clock on the sun?* I am asking an improper and absurd question. Most philosophical questions are equally absurd according to the Analytical School.

It thus came to be claimed that language alone formed the entire subject-matter of philosophy, and analysis of language became the key to metaphysical truth. Of course many philosophers, very notably Plato, had regarded language as an important *part* of the philosopher's business, but this was the first time that philosophy was reduced to linguistic analysis and nothing else.

This does not mean that philosophical problems are *about* language; of course they are not, they are about knowledge, truth, mind and matter; what is urged is, however, that these problems spring *from* language, reveal confusion as to the uses of language, and are to be solved, *or removed*, by employing language properly.

MIND AND MATTER

Among the problems which disappear, says Professor Ayer, are those " concerning the possibility of bridging the gulf between mind and matter "—the conflict between idealists who reduce all material things to minds, and materialists who treat thought not as a substance but as the function of the brain.   This basic question in philosophy is ruled out as not really within its province and as not capable of being rationally discussed.

An excellent example of the linguistic approach to this problem will be found in Gilbert Ryle's *The Concept of Mind*. Ryle says that a whole host of meaningless and futile questions as to the relation of mind to matter have arisen because of what he calls ' the dogma of the Ghost in the Machine '— the view that mind is a spiritual substance inhabiting a material body.   He regards this basic error as linguistic and his book is a classical example of the new method in operation.

This question was dealt with by Aristotle and Aquinas in quite a different way when they argued that mind was a function of the brain and not a substance, and the same argument has been used by many other philosophers—most recently by Whitehead.   If this approach helps us to surmount the problem, has it been discussed and settled *linguistically*, or by the normal process of rational argument without any concern with language as such ?   Critics of Logical Analysis would deny that it is a linguistic problem at all. It is rather a question of getting hold of the right end of the stick.

THE RIGHT END OF THE STICK

There are a great many philosophical problems (and ethical, scientific, political and economic problems too) which are indeed the result of muddled thinking, of approaching a problem from the wrong point of view.[1] Under these circumstances the inquirer is baffled and confused, he feels that he doesn't know his way about, as when his philosophy tells him that something is true that he simply cannot believe, such as denying the existence of the material world. Now the right approach in such dilemmas is not to hammer away at the problem *as stated*, because the reason why there is no solution, or that there is an absurd one, is precisely that it is stated wrongly. This was clearly seen when we traced the mentalism of Berkeley back to the theory of representative perception in Descartes and Locke. The solution is found by approaching the problem in a different way.

One of the principal tasks of philosophy is, therefore, to recast insoluble problems, to pick up the right end of the stick. " To show the fly the way out of the bottle."

Many philosophical problems do not have to be solved. They dissolve. They are not real questions, but *muddles felt as problems*, which wither away when the ground is cleared. Philosophy can only advance when such problems are removed, only then can it proceed to its constructive tasks. Philosophy's first achievement is as a fog dispeller.

VERIFIABILITY

The demand of Analytical philosophers, that all statements must be capable of verification, can and should be extended and clarified, it will then be found to be useful. If we regard, as we should, philosophical explanations as hypotheses, then we should remember that no hypothesis has any significance unless it can be tested, unless, that is to say, there could be facts which refute it.

This is useful not only in science but when dealing with such theories as Bergson's vitalism. Suppose every puzzle in biology and evolution is explained by appealing to a vital

[1] Professor Butterfield has an interesting discussion on this as it is found in the history of science in his book, *The Origins of Modern Science.*

force, what is wrong with the whole approach? It is that the hypothesis is consistent with any facts whatsoever. What explains everything explains nothing. Compare the theory of evolution with this. There are many possible facts that could disprove it—fossils of vertebrates in the earliest strata, for instance. But the facts which would overthrow the theory are not forthcoming; on the contrary, more and more facts support it, therefore the theory becomes more and more probable.

The principle of verifiability by further observation and experiment can be extended to many problems such as that of the existence of evil, a providential order in the world, mind as a substance, and so on. When this is done it will be found that there is a class of metaphysical theories in relation to which facts can be advanced neither to support them nor in evidence against them. It is such theories that are unverifiable and meaningless. But there are other metaphysical theories, explanatory hypotheses, and interpretations of life which can be either supported or contradicted by facts. These are meaningful and can reasonably be discussed.

PHILOSOPHY AND THE ANGLE OF VISION

Philosophy is many things, and there is no formula to cover them all. But if I were asked to express in one single word what is its most essential feature I would unhesitatingly say: Vision. There is something visionary about great metaphysicians as if they had the power to see beyond the horizons of their time,

says Professor Waismann, one of our most persuasive contemporary philosophers.[1]

What do we mean by vision? Vision is a new way of seeing, and what goes with it, the will to transform the whole intellectual scene. This is true of scientific theories, but it

[1] F. Waismann, *Contemporary British Philosophy.*

is also true of metaphysical systems like that of Aristotle and Thomas Aquinas, Descartes and Spinoza. What every philosopher is trying to do is to win people over from the conventional outlook to a new way of looking at things, to change the whole climate of opinion. This was especially true of the philosophers who followed Galileo and Copernicus and those who followed Darwin. It is true also of the successors of Hegel; not of those who elaborated his doctrines into ever-deepening obscurity, but of the historians and sociologists whom he taught to find in the passage of time not merely a succession of independent episodes, but intelligible processes of change, of growth and decay, of renewal and reorganisation.

What systems of thought, what speculative vision do we find in our world today? The three most significant, which may be reasonably associated with metaphysics, are : (a) The *Scholastic Philosophy* of *Thomas Aquinas*, influential in the Catholic world and beyond it, (b) *Absolute Idealism* as reflected in the great religions of India and in all forms of mysticism, (c) *Evolutionary Naturalism*, as the world view of many scientists who do not accept either of the two former systems.

SCHOLASTICISM

This great system, which reigned supreme in western Europe for many centuries, still offers a rational and comprehensive system based on belief in God, whose existence is held to be capable of proof by the argument for a First Cause. It is a system to which reason points, but which is accepted on faith, and thereafter provides a system of doctrine which, though rational, is inaccessible to reason. The vision which the Church grants, although based on a rational theology, is embodied in rites and ceremonies, pictures and the sacred drama, music, poetry and literature, thus presenting itself in a way to appeal to every side of human nature. One of the most powerful arguments for its truth is that it so perfectly fits the human condition and its varied needs. As Chesterton says :

> When once these two parts of the two machines had come together, one after another, all the other parts fitted and fell in with an eerie exactitude. I could hear bolt after bolt over all the machinery falling into its place with a kind of click of relief. Having got one part right, all the other parts were repeating that rectitude, as clock after clock strikes noon. Instinct after instinct was answered by doctrine after doctrine.[1]

ABSOLUTE IDEALISM

We have already discussed the idealism of the followers of Hegel. Something rather similar was held, not simply as a creed, but as a vision of the ultimate meaning of life, by Plotinus and the great Christian mystics, and is also found in Brahmanism, the philosophical theology of the Hindu religion, and in what Aldous Huxley calls " The Perennial Philosophy ".

Such philosophies hold that ultimate reality, which endures and forms the substraction of all outward and changing forms, is diffused through the universe, yet present in every individual. The world is illusion ; life is evil and obscures our real unity with the Absolute. The goal of existence for the individual is release from the endless series of reincarnations so that we sink at last into the universal self.

EVOLUTIONARY NATURALISM

This philosophy, which has a certain kinship with Spinozism and even with certain aspects of Aristotelianism, puts man and his experience squarely into the Nature over against which he has hitherto been set. The obliteration of this gulf was achieved by the discovery of biological evolution.

[1] G. K. Chesterton, *Orthodoxy*.

Naturalism is opposed to all dualism between Nature and another realm of being, the supernatural. Its faith is in the power of life to establish and magnify itself through the progressive mastery of the environment.

Marxism may be held to be a form of evolutionary naturalism with a strong admixture of Hegelian dialectic and a polemical political application. Briefly it seeks to achieve in society what Darwin saw happening in nature, the modification of structure to adapt it better to the demands of the environment. Marx believed that the great development of the productive forces under capitalism demanded a drastic modification of society to adapt it to the changed conditions of monopoly capitalism. But he saw this as taking place not through variation and inheritance but as involving social conflict and conscious political activity.[1]

DOES IT WORK?

Of all such visions or speculative metaphysical systems two questions may be asked:

(1) Do they work? (2) Are they true?

The answer to the first question is historical and empirical. It may also be highly controversial. It is, however, properly related to philosophical inquiry if we consider the question of 'working' pragmatically. For the pragmatist, what works in any sense, what is expedient in any way, is true to that extent. Critics of pragmatism disagree. They are prepared to say that if a theory is true it must work, but they do not admit that everything that works is true.[2] And if by working we mean what James means, that it *satisfies*, then no psychologist would for a moment allow that what satisfies human wishes is true. It is as often quite the contrary.

[1] The ethical and political questions involved are of immense importance, but are distinct from the philosophical basis.

[2] The theory of the 'ether' as a mysterious 'something' in which waves could be formed, *worked* as an explanation of how light was transmitted, but has been disproved.

A second way in which a theory might be held to work is that suggested in Chesterton's *Orthodoxy*, namely, that it neatly fits all the scattered facts into a rational picture. The difficulty is that several totally inconsistent pictures, or mythologies, or systems of thought, can do that, for instance, Idealism, Spinozism, the theory of Leibniz, the system of Aquinas. All these have satisfied thoughtful people as able to explain all the facts. How are we to choose between them except on purely personal grounds, which is thoroughly unsatisfactory? We are again driven back to the question of truth.

IS IT TRUE?

(*a*) Philosophy throws some light on this question by distinguishing between the *necessary* and the *sufficient*. It is *necessary* to be at least 18 years old to enter a university, but that is not a *sufficient* reason for being admitted. There are other qualifications. Now it is necessary that a true theory should (i) work, (ii) link up the facts, but neither (nor both together) offers a *sufficient reason* for accepting its truth.

(*b*) Dewey has pointed out that a theory is essentially *a guide to action*. The object of intelligent conduct, that is to say, conduct guided by a rational view of things, is to discover forms of action by which all the values of life are extended and rendered more secure, including the diffusion of the fine arts and the cultivation of taste, the processes of education and all activities concerned with rendering human relationships more significant and worthy. Problem solving solutions, in this sense (and not meaning solutions of mere intellectual puzzles) have a *claim* to truth, to ' warranted assertibility '.

(*c*) A criterion accepted by many philosophers is the rejection of all theories or explanations which offer vital forces, mysterious entities and agencies, and of all animistic ways of thinking. This would not rule out the First Cause argument on the one hand, or Absolute Idealism on the other, but it would rule out Vitalism.

(d) A criterion that has been advanced by many modern philosophers is that the truth of no belief can be demonstrated if it is so conceived as to be compatible with no matter what facts of observation; no theory can be considered which is not in principle capable of some test in actual experience. It must be possible to recognise the state of affairs which would prove the theory and the state of affairs that would disprove it.

This argument has been levelled against Absolute Idealism, since no matter how much evil there is in the world the theory is totally unaffected on the ground that " the very presence of evil in the temporal order is the condition of the perfection of the eternal order ".[1] Here, then, is a theory that is neither confirmed nor contradicted by any facts whatsoever. Such a theory, it is held, cannot be offered as a candidate for a rational world view.

L. WITTGENSTEIN (1889–1951)

Russell's analytical method had a profound effect on a young Austrian who came to Trinity College, Cambridge in 1912. Wittgenstein's conclusion, which carried him beyond Russell's own position, was embodied in a revolutionary philosophical work, *Tractatus Logico-Philosophicus* (1921), which made a considerable impact upon a circle of philosophers mainly interested in the basic theories of science, known as the Vienna Circle. Here analysis took a trend in the direction of developing the logic of scientific method, known as Logical Positivism, which accepted Russell's view and that of the *Tractatus* that valid scientific statements must be based on empirical observations. All other statements were rejected as metaphysical. These philosophers demanded factual verification for every statement made,

[1] Josiah Royce, *The World and the Individual.*

holding that for a belief to have any meaning it must be in principle capable of being tested by observation and experiment. *Analysis*, for them, becomes the method of stating the criteria for distinguishing meaningful statements from the multitude of unverifiable claims and propositions.

This group of scientists and logicians with the coming of fascism dispersed, some of them coming to England, but most of them going to America. In England their position was eloquently and forcefully stated by the Oxford logician A. J. Ayer in his *Language, Truth and Logic*. At this stage it came to be known as Logical Positivism, which held that what could not be verified by observation must be rejected as metaphysical. Thus most of the traditional philosophical questions were thought of as meaningless since whether they were the case or not made no difference to the facts of the world, which they purported to 'explain'. The discussion of such questions was held to be a mistake, and Wittgenstein's approach was designed to 'cure' philosophers who asked them of a kind of mental cramp, and to persuade them in future to concern themselves only with 'what could be said', i.e., what could be verified or disverified by appeal to factual evidence.

But Wittgenstein himself grew profoundly dissatisfied with his own position as expounded in the *Tractatus*, for what he had written there now appeared to him to fall under the condemnation of all statements which cannot be verified by reference to observed facts, about which nothing can be said. One cannot *say* anything about "the agreement of a proposition with reality", for any propositions which attempt to say what this agreement is are not in themselves statements of empirical fact. Wittgenstein concludes that *the formula which states the criterion of what is a meaningful statement is thus not itself a verifiable proposition*.

Wittgenstein now proceeded to develop an entirely new kind of analysis, which became known as *linguistic analysis*.

Like Russell and the Vienna positivists, he found no sense in propositions or even problems of a philosophical sort; but he no longer concerned himself with problems about how meaningful language can be made to conform to a world of facts. He concerned himself only with *language itself,* regarding any question about the relation of language to the reality which it describes as unnecessary and unphilosophical. Thus philosophy changes its role. It does not answer philosophical problems, it removes them from the agenda. If we use words correctly and not metaphysically nor in other ways which give rise to fictitious problems, we can get along perfectly well. There is nothing for philosophy to reveal. It " leaves everything as it is ".

But this position, either in the earlier form (logical positivism) or Wittgenstein's later *linguistic* form, appeared to provide no justification for scientific laws as really explanatory, as going beyond the data to theories which cannot be reached by pure logic—a position formerly supported by both Hume and Russell. Must they be blindly accepted as an act of faith?

LINGUISTIC ANALYSIS

We have seen that Wittgenstein abandoned the conviction that language *must* refer to concrete facts. Meaning is now seen to be *not* asking what the terms refer to. Many terms in our conversation *don't* refer to facts; they may express my hope, my disappointment, my anger, a request, my approval. These are not observable facts, like tables and chairs. Wittgenstein found that there were different *modes* of speaking, just as we use a different language when we are talking about chess from when we are talking about football. It is quite easy to find out how words are being used. It is no philosophical puzzle; just look and see what we actually mean when we say, for instance, that ' *democracy* ' really means this or that. For when we speak like that we are not doing the same thing as when we say " *that* is St. Paul's Cathedral ", pointing to it.   What we are saying about ' *democracy* ' is really that we should like everyone to agree with what we think it really is.   We are speaking not descriptively but *persuasively*.

Thus Wittgenstein makes no effort either to *describe* the world, or to explain it or criticise it.   This is not the purpose of thought.   The world is what it is; and the meaning of our phrases can be found from seeing how in fact we use them. Nothing more has to be understood or explained.

But Wittgenstein was also anxious to point out that every generally accepted way of speaking really represents a way of life—such as the language and phrases of ' hippies ', of army officers, of coal miners, even of religious people does. Of course, if you try to understand the hippy in terms of the world of the army officer you won't get very far!

But is there any criterion for ruling out one or other whole way of speaking, say religion?   Not unless you make religion a philosophical explanation of the world.   This is to go beyond the scope of language altogether.   It can only be descriptive, or simply reflect our religious feelings and *point of view*.   The notion of philosophical truth is ' out '.

Mathematical truth, of course, like abstract knowledge, is something different.   It isn't about the world at all.   It never states more than: *if* a certain group of symbols is examined it *implies* a further symbolic expression.   This is the only necessary truth that there is, and it is ' computer ' truth, a logical mechanism with which to juggle with facts which you feed into it.   But as Russell said of mathematics, and it is true of formal logic too, " In mathematics we never know what we are talking about, or whether what we say is true ".

Linguistic analysis became the orthodoxy of a whole generation of philosophers, but there were always critics, like Russell, and today there can be either a rejection of its claims in modern terms or a return to the older and more comprehensive intellectual attitude of classical philosophy.

AGAINST LINGUISTICS

(a) Russell said that:

> The new philosophy seems to me to have abandoned, without necessity, that grave and important task which philosophy throughout the ages has hitherto pursued. Philosophers have tried to understand the world. . . . I cannot feel that the new philosophy is carrying on this tradition.[1]

(b) Professor Karl Popper holds that the whole enterprise is misguided. It is for ever sharpening the knife, and never cutting anything.

> I have spectacles, and I am cleaning my spectacles now. But spectacles have a *function*, and they function only when you put them on to look through them *at the world*. It is the same with language.[2]

Popper criticised the linguistic philosophers for being ignorant of science and uninterested in history and politics. He spoke of the whole tendency as intellectual suicide.

THOMAS KUHN AND THE PARADIGM SHIFT

A severe blow was dealt against all who believe that the world must be taken as it is, and that common ways of feeling and thinking must be our only test of truth by Thomas Kuhn. In his *Structure of Scientific Revolutions* (1962) Kuhn points out that the whole of human thought proceeds by radical re-structuring, the changing of all our basic concepts. This happened when the earth was no longer

[1] Russell, *My Philosophical Development*.
[2] Popper in the BBC Interview with Strawson and Warnock.

believed to be the centre of the universe. Darwin's evolutionary theory would be another example. The history of science is one long story of intellectual 'shifts' of patterns, of basic theory. Kuhn called this ' paradigm shift ' and it applies also to basic points of view about life and history and economics.

Thus, one cannot accept as final any view of the world that assures us that ' everything is as it is '. On the contrary, the history of philosophy is the history of radical changes in our point of view. These, says Kuhn, take place when the older order or pattern of thought becomes riddled with anomalies and contradictions. There are critical thinkers today who see our generally accepted world in just that condition, and are anticipating in philosophy and history, and our whole world picture, ' a paradigm shift '.

Kuhn points out that it is seldom that one whole world view, such as Newton's or Darwin's, can be proved so conclusively that it overcomes the older one once and for all. The battle is not won by proofs but by the growth of a *consensus* of scientific opinion supporting the new theory. Old philosophies never die; like old soldiers, they just fade away.

KARL POPPER

Fortunately there is a more satisfactory way of dealing with this difficulty which has been proposed by Karl Popper and has secured wide support among scientists.

Popper abandoned altogether the attempt to *justify* induction logically, as misguided and involving one inevitably in an infinite regress in the search for certainty. He directed attention to the importance of methods not of establishing, but of refuting or *falsifying,* general laws and explanatory theories. A well-formulated scientific law or theory is always consistent with the observations on which it has been based, therefore such consistency does not prove it—but it must also be so formulated as to make clear what sort of facts would be inconsistent with it, i.e. what future observations would falsify it. Theories are *tested* by making every effort by systematic observation and experiment to falsify them. And they can be regarded as established so far, and only so far, as they have remained unfalsified. This procedure of testing theories by efforts to falsify them can never reach any absolute certainty as regards the truth of any theory. But scientists do not require in establishing a law or theory the certainty that is proper to mathematical deduction.

Deduction of that kind is indispensable *within* science, but its laws and theories are not *reached* by any such process. And science does very well with the relative truth of hypotheses that have been pretty thoroughly tested and up to a point verified, even though this falls short of absolute finality. This means of course that all such theories are open to revision, modification and sometimes to complete reformulation.

Popper's approach to the problem is based on the fact that no matter how many instances we can find that are consistent with the law or theory under discussion, they do not conclusively verify it; but *one* case inconsistent with the law refutes it. If, therefore, you frame a hypothesis which recognises and states what facts *would* refute it, and then test it and find that nothing happens to refute it, it begins to look like truth. Theories cannot be completely verified, but they can be falsified by a single negative instance. The more possible cases there are where a statement *could* be refuted by the evidence, but in fact isn't, the more reason do we have to treat it as possessing a useful degree of truth.

THE TEST OF A PHILOSOPHY

It must be for the student of philosophy himself to seek to apply these tests to those philosophies which seem to him worthy of investigation, and, what is even more important, to devote his thought to devising better ones.   If a philosophy is primarily the kind of understanding of the world that guides our actions and fulfils our needs, its value will lie in the success it brings in enabling us to deal with the existing situation; so that the final justification of all ideas, like their meaning, is to be found less in their logical structure than in the service they render in the battle of life.

A world view, it would seem, should be considered in the light of such considerations as these: Does it end in conclusions which, when they are referred back to ordinary life-experiences and their predicaments, render them more significant, more luminous to us, and make our dealings with them more fruitful?   Or does it terminate in rendering the things of ordinary experience more opaque than they were before, and in depriving them of having in ' reality ' even the significance they had previously seemed to have?   Does it yield the enrichment and increase of power of ordinary things which the results of physical science afford when applied in everyday affairs?   Or does it become a mystery that these ordinary things should be what they are, or indeed that they should be at all, while philosophic concepts are left to dwell in separation in some realm of their own?   It is the fact that so many philosophies terminate in conclusions that make it necessary to disparage and condemn primary experience, leading those who hold them to measure the sublimity of their ' realities ', as philosophically defined, by remoteness from the concerns of daily life, which leads common sense to look askance at philosophy.

But if philosophy gathers from the philosophy of the past its rich harvest of human wisdom and insight, its store of human experience, incorporating in its more critical conclusions and more adequate framework the facts and experiences they emphasised, it will recommend the philosopher's task to the plain man and in its light " the wayfaring man though a fool shall not err therein ".

Books for Further Reading

ONE of the best biographical histories of philosophy is
Will Durant's *Story of Philosophy* (Benn). A book which
very fairly and lucidly discusses the way in which different
philosophies deal with basic problems is Hocking's *Types of
Philosophy* (Scribners). Many will wish to turn to Bertrand
Russell's *History of Western Philosophy*. It contains many
brilliant pages, but the reader is likely to find too much
space devoted to medieval philosophy and too little to those
philosophers, like Kant, whom Russell does not like. An
important background book is Randall's *Making of the Modern
Mind* (Allen & Unwin).

There is now available an excellent series of paper-backs.
Of these, one of the best is *The Mentor Philosophers*: (1) The
Age of Belief, (2) The Age of Adventure, (3) The Age of
Reason, (4) The Age of Enlightenment, (5) The Age of
Analysis. Each volume contains an introductory essay and
then selections from the philosophers of the period with an
introduction to each.

Paper-back editions of most of the philosophical classics
are now available, many of them published in the United
States, but available at such bookshops as Foyle's. Penguin
Books have produced an excellent series of books by contemporary philosophers on the great names of philosophy;
of these Hampshire's *Spinoza* can be specially recommended.

The Analytical School is frequently very difficult, but
Ayer's *Language, Truth and Logic* (Gollancz) is brilliantly
written, and D. J. O'Connor has very lucidly summed up
the position of this school in *The Philosophy of Education*

(Routledge), which in spite of its title really goes to the heart of philosophical analysis.

From a different point of view the historical approach will be found in the *Introduction to Philosophy* (Watts) by John Lewis, who has also dealt with the importance of a World View in his *Science, Faith and Scepticism* (Lawrence & Wishart).

There is a very clear account of Wittgenstein in *Wittgenstein and Modern Philosophy*, by Justus Hartnack (Methuen), and a brilliant criticism of both the logical positivists and linguistic analyses by Ernest Gellner, *Words and Things* (Gollancz). There is no short book on Popper, but from libraries it should be possible to obtain a volume of his essays called *Conjectures and Refutations* (Routledge).   Finally I can recommend a clear and simple introduction to the approach of the Ayer-Wittgenstein school in its most modern form.   This is *Thinking Philosophically* by Frederick Vivian (Chatto and Windus).

Index